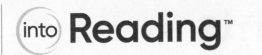

Guiding Principles and Strategies

Grades 3–5

D1404450

Printed in the U.S.A.

ISBN   978-1-328-58168-6

3 4 5 6 7 8 9 10   0868   27 26 25 24 23 22 21 20 19

4500788272   ^ B C D E F G

Table of Contents

TEACHING AND LEARNING

Foundations and Best Practices

¡VIVA EL ESPAÑOL!

Dear Teachers:

Thank you! Thank you for opening the minds of all of the students who will walk into your classroom this year, next year, and in the many years to come. Both of us had children who would sometimes slip and call a favorite teacher "Mom" or "Dad" because our children, just like your students, learn from you, depend on you, turn to you, and do indeed sometimes see you as that other parent-figure in their lives. You are an integral part of the students you teach, and we thank you for all that you do.

We're excited to be, in a small way, a part of that teacher-student relationship through our work on *Into Reading*, a reading program that excites us both. With a new vision for how to bring reading into students' lives, this program breaks boundaries. Filled with award-winning literature, familiar classics, and newer stories that represent the great diversity of this nation and world, these texts will become touchstones in a child's reading life. Students will write directly in their books, making them their very own. Students will take their books home to read to their mom or dad, their abuela or abuelo. And as *Into Reading* inspires a love of reading, it will lead students to deeper close reading so that they can become the engaged, attentive, critical readers we want all students to be.

We're especially excited that our Notice and Note protocol is a part of this program. If you're still learning about this protocol, you'll soon discover that it offers readers the "signposts" they must recognize to understand the author's theme in works of fiction, or the author's purpose in works of nonfiction. You'll discover that your students can successfully analyze a text once they've learned to identify and use these signposts. And you'll watch with pride as your students discover that when they get into reading, doors open, windows widen, and the horizon is theirs.

Each day for your students is a new wonder. We're excited to be on this journey with you as you and your students step *Into Reading*. The stories, the information, the excitement, the learning, and the joy of reading all come together with this program, your students, and your teaching. Let's begin!

Kylene Beers
Bob Probst

Kylene and Bob
Into Reading and *¡Arriba la Lectura!* Authors

A comprehensive literacy solution based on science and informed by teachers

Student-Centered Instructional Design

A flexible, balanced approach with a focus on small-group instruction to develop collaborative, self-directed learners

Data-Driven Differentiation

Planning, grouping, and assessment tools that allow teachers to focus on delivering individualized instruction

Equity for Dual Language Instruction

A research-based and fully equitable Spanish solution for developing biliteracy in dual language classrooms

A Robust Library

Captivating content and high-quality texts that strengthen students' skills and ignite a lifelong love of learning

Social-Emotional Development

Embedded support for development of the whole child with a focus on social-emotional learning and growth mindset

Family and Community Partnerships

Resources that honor families as an integral part of the learning process and extend learning beyond the classroom

Get Into Reading!

Grades 3, 4, and 5 of *Into Reading* and *¡Arriba la lectura!* are each organized into 12 modules. Students build knowledge as they read about, write about, view, and discuss each module topic.

¡Arriba la Lectura! cuenta con todo esto y más. En la sección ¡Viva el español! verá lo que distingue a este programa.

GRADE 3 Overview	**1** What a Character!	**2** Use Your Words	**3** Let Freedom Ring!
? ESSENTIAL QUESTION	**What makes a character interesting?**	**How do people use words to express themselves?**	**How do historic places, documents, and symbols represent our nation?**
MODULE FOCUS	📖 **LANGUAGE ARTS:** Characters	📖 **LANGUAGE ARTS:** Words	🌐 **SOCIAL STUDIES:** U.S. History
⚙ LEARNING MINDSET	**Belonging**	**Seeking Challenges**	**Grit**
TEXT SETS	**WEEK 1** • *Calamity Jane* • *Zach Jumps In!* • *The Elephant Moon of Sir Herbert Spoon* • *Marisol McDonald Doesn't Match! / ¡Marisol McDonald no combina!* **WEEK 2** • *Judy Moody Mood Martian* • *Stink and the Freaky Frog Freakout* **WEEK 3** • *Scaredy Squirrel* • *Weslandia*	**WEEK 1** • *Use Your Words* • *A LOL Story* • *Wordy Birds* • *Dear Primo* **WEEK 2** • *Adventures with Words* • *The Upside Down Boy / El niño de cabeza* **WEEK 3** • *Dear Dragon* • *The Lemonade War*	**WEEK 1** • *American Landmarks* • *American Places, American Ideals* • *Patriotic Tunes* • *The U.S. Constitution* **WEEK 2** • *Why We Celebrate the Fourth of July* • *The Flag Maker* **WEEK 3** • *Why Is the Statue of Liberty Green?* • *All the Places to Love*
⬇ WRITING FORM	**Personal Narrative**	**Letter**	**Descriptive Essay**

4 Stories on Stage	5 Teamwork	6 Animal Behaviors
Why might some stories be better told as plays?	What can sports teach us about working together?	What behaviors help animals survive?
📖 LANGUAGE ARTS: Drama	🌐 SOCIAL STUDIES: Teamwork	🌱 SCIENCE: Animal Survival
Self-Reflection	Asking for Help	Noticing
WEEK 1 • *Auditions* • *That's Entertainment!* • *The Lion King's Friend* • *The Saga of Pecos Bill*	**WEEK 1** • *How Do We Win?* • *Teamwork = Victory!* • *Competition, Cooperation – and FUN!* • *Soccer Shootout*	**WEEK 1** • *Shall We Dance?* • *Frozen Alive* • *Living Glass* • *This Is Your Life Cycle*
WEEK 2 • *The Traveling Trio* • *Gigi and the Wishing Ring*	**WEEK 2** • *Bend It Like Bianca* • *Running Rivals*	**WEEK 2** • *The Nose Awards* • *Octopus Escapes Again*
WEEK 3 • *Two Bear Cubs* • *Crossing Bok Chitto*	**WEEK 3** • *Brothers at Bat* • *Don't Feed the Geckos!*	**WEEK 3** • *T.J. The Siberian Tiger Cub* • *In November*
Story	**Persuasive Letter**	**Expository Essay**

WELCOME TO *INTO READING*

GRADE 3 Overview *(cont.)*	⑦ Make a Difference	⑧ Imagine! Invent!	⑨ From Farm to Table
❓ ESSENTIAL QUESTION	How can one person make a meaningful difference in their local or global community?	What does it take to make a successful invention?	How does food get to your table?
MODULE FOCUS	🌐 **SOCIAL STUDIES:** Community	🌱 **SCIENCE:** Inventions	🌱 **SCIENCE:** Farming
LEARNING MINDSET	**Purpose**	**Problem Solving**	**Planning Ahead**
TEXT SETS	**WEEK 1** • *Kids Change the World* • *Let's Build a Park!* • *The Eco-Troubador* • *Farmer Will Allen and the Growing Table* **WEEK 2** • *One Plastic Bag* • *Energy Island* **WEEK 3** • *The Storyteller's Candle / La Velita De Los Cuentos* • *What If Everybody Did That?*	**WEEK 1** • *Getting There* • *A Century of Amazing Inventions* • *(Some of) the Greatest Inventions* • *Timeless Thomas* **WEEK 2** • *A Bumpy Ride* • *Rosie Revere, Engineer* **WEEK 3** • *Edison's Best Invention* • *Now & Ben*	**WEEK 1** • *From Corn to Pop* • *Great Ideas from Great Parents!* • *Lobster Bait* • *How Did That Get in My Lunchbox?* **WEEK 2** • *Carrots, Farm to Fork* • *How Do You Raise a Raisin?* **WEEK 3** • *It's Our Garden* • *Gone Fishing*
📖 WRITING FORM	**Opinion Essay**	**Research Report**	**Poem**

10 Tell a Tale	**11** Genre Study: Nonfiction	**12** Genre Study: Literary Texts
Why is it important to pass stories down to the next generation?	What are the characteristics of informational text, narrative nonfiction, and opinion text?	What are the characteristics of realistic fiction, poetry, and traditional tales?
🌐 SOCIAL STUDIES: Cultural Tales	WEEK 1 Informational Text WEEK 2 Narrative Nonfiction WEEK 3 Opinion Text	WEEK 1 Realistic Fiction WEEK 2 Poetry WEEK 3 Traditional Tales
Perseverance	**Growth Mindset**	**Resilience**

Tell a Tale — Perseverance

WEEK 1
- *Tortoise and Hare*
- *Why We Share Stories*
- *Aesop's Fables*
- *When the Giant Stirred*

WEEK 2
- *Why the Sky Is Far Away*
- *Cinder Al and the Stinky Footwear*

WEEK 3
- 🌐 *Compay Mono y Comay Jicotea*
- *The Plot Chickens*

Genre Study: Nonfiction — Growth Mindset

WEEK 1
- *The U.S. Constitution*
- *The Nose Awards*
- *T.J. The Siberian Tiger Cub*
- *Timeless Thomas*
- *A Bumpy Ride*
- *How Did That Get in My Lunchbox?*
- *It's Our Garden*

WEEK 2
- 🌐 *The Upside Down Boy / El nino de cabeza*
- *The Flag Maker*
- *Why Is the Statue of Liberty Green?*
- *Brothers at Bat*
- *This Is Your Life Cycle*
- *Octopus Escapes Again!*
- *Energy Island*

WEEK 3
- *That's Entertainment!*
- *Let's Build a Park!*
- *Edison's Best Invention*
- *Great Ideas from Great Parents!*

Genre Study: Literary Texts — Resilience

WEEK 1
- 🌐 *Marisol McDonald Doesn't Match! / ¡Marisol McDonald no combina!*
- *Judy Moody Mood Martian*
- *Stink and the Freaky Frog Freakout*
- *Dear Primo*
- *Soccer Shootout*
- *Running Rivals*

WEEK 2
- *Adventures with Words*
- *Dear Dragon*
- *Rosie Revere, Engineer*
- *How Do You Raise a Raisin?*

WEEK 3
- *The Saga of Pecos Bill*
- *Gigi and the Wishing Ring*
- *Two Bear Cubs*
- *When the Giant Stirred*
- *Why the Sky Is Far Away*
- 🌐 *Compay Mono y Comay Jicotea*

Imaginative Story	**Persuasive Essay**	**Biographical Essay**

Get Into Reading!

Grades 3, 4, and 5 of *Into Reading* and *¡Arriba la lectura!* are each organized into 12 modules. Students build knowledge as they read about, write about, view, and discuss each module topic.

¡Arriba la Lectura!
cuenta con todo esto y más.
En la sección ¡Viva el español!
verá lo que distingue a
este programa.

GRADE 4 Overview	**①** What Makes Us Who We Are?	**②** Come to Your Senses	**③** Rise to the Occasion
? ESSENTIAL QUESTION	How do your experiences help shape your identity?	How do people and animals use their senses to navigate the world?	What does it take to meet a challenge?
MODULE FOCUS	🌐 SOCIAL STUDIES: Personal Experiences	🌱 SCIENCE: The Five Senses	🌐 SOCIAL STUDIES: Challenges
⚙ LEARNING MINDSET	Growth Mindset	Noticing	Seeking Challenges
TEXT SETS	**WEEK 1** • *Life* • *The Story of You* • *Michael's Melody* • *Flora & Ulysses: The Illuminated Adventures* **WEEK 2** • *Yes! We Are Latinos* • *The Year of the Rat* **WEEK 3** • *Kitoto the Mighty* • *La Mariposa*	**WEEK 1** • *Super Senses* • *What Are the Five Senses?* • *The Man Who Climbed Everest* • *The Science Behind Sight* **WEEK 2** • *Animal Senses* • *Blind Ambition* **WEEK 3** • *The Game of Silence* • *Apex Predators*	**WEEK 1** • *Rise Up* • *Never Give Up!* • *Ellen Ochoa* • *Rent Party Jazz* **WEEK 2** • *The Galveston Hurricane of 1900* • *Catch Me If You Can* **WEEK 3** • *My Diary from Here to There / Mi diario de aqui hasta allá* • *The Kite Fighters*
⬇ WRITING FORM	Personal Narrative	Description	Opinion Essay

4 Heroic Feats	**5** Art Everywhere	**6** Marvels of Nature
What makes someone a hero?	How far can your talents take you?	What makes Earth's natural wonders exciting and unique?
🌐 **SOCIAL STUDIES:** Goals	🌐 **SOCIAL STUDIES:** The Arts	🌱 **SCIENCE:** Earth's Natural Wonders
Resilience	**Belonging**	**Wonder**

WEEK 1 • *Everyday Heroes* • *Who's a Hero?* • *Mack and the Hidden Tree House* • *Prince Charming Misplaces His Bride*	**WEEK 1** • *Art for All* • *Why Art Centers Matter* • *Carmen Lomas Garza: Bringing Memories to Life* • *The Beatles Were Fab (and They Were Funny)*	**WEEK 1** • *Amazing Planet Earth* • *Seven Natural Wonders* • *Incredible Waterfalls* • *Mariana Trench*
WEEK 2 • *Smokejumpers to the Rescue!* • *Perseus and the Fall of Medusa*	**WEEK 2** • *How Can Photos Take Us Back in Time?* • *Let's Dance Around the World*	**WEEK 2** • *Weird and Wondrous Rocks* • *Nature's Wonders*
WEEK 3 • *The Battle of the Alamo* • *Love Will See You Through*	**WEEK 3** • *The Art of Poetry* • *Mejor diversion, Agua quieta* • *Mr. Ferris and His Wheel*	**WEEK 3** • *Grand Canyon: A Trail Through Time* • *Coral Reefs*
Story	**Expository Essay**	**Letter**

GRADE 4 Overview *(cont.)*	**7** Tricksters and Tall Tales	**8** Food for Thought	**9** Global Guardians
ESSENTIAL QUESTION	What lessons can you learn from characters in traditional tales?	What can we do to make more healthful food choices?	What can people do to care for our planet?
MODULE FOCUS	SOCIAL STUDIES: Traditional Stories	SCIENCE: Nutrition	SCIENCE: Conservation
LEARNING MINDSET	Self-Reflection	Planning Ahead	Grit
TEXT SETS	**WEEK 1** • *A Poor, Defenseless Wolf* • *A Tale of Traditional Tales* • *Anaya* • *Thunder Rose* **WEEK 2** • *In the Days of King Adobe / En los días del Rey Adobín* • *A Pair of Tricksters* **WEEK 3** • *Ten Suns (a Chinese legend); The Ten Suns* • *The Luck of the Loch Ness Monster*	**WEEK 1** • *Cupcake vs. Apple* • *To Your Health!* • *Not So Sweet* • *Eco-Friendly Food* **WEEK 2** • *Kids Rock Nutrition in the Kitchen* • *Bug Bites* **WEEK 3** • *Now You're Cooking!* • *It's Disgusting and We Ate It!*	**WEEK 1** • *Young Guardians* • *The Eco Guardians* • *The Lifecycle of Trash* • *Luz Sees the Light* **WEEK 2** • *On Sea Turtle Patrol* • *How Can We Reduce Household Waste?* **WEEK 3** • *Seeds of Change* • *The Case of the Vanishing Honeybees*
WRITING FORM	**Imaginative Story**	**Opinion Essay**	**Research Report**

(10) Communication Nation	(11) Genre Study: Nonfiction	(12) Genre Study: Literary Texts
What forms can communication take?	**What are the characteristics of informational text, biography, and argumentative text?**	**What are the characteristics of realistic fiction, traditional tales, and historical fiction?**
🌐 SOCIAL STUDIES: Communication	WEEK 1 Informational Text WEEK 2 Biography WEEK 3 Argumentative Text	WEEK 1 Realistic Fiction WEEK 2 Traditional Tales WEEK 3 Historical Fiction
Problem Solving	**Problem Solving**	**Noticing**

Communication Nation	Genre Study: Nonfiction	Genre Study: Literary Texts
WEEK 1 • *Born to Communicate* • *How Technology Has Changed Communication* • *The Unbroken Code of the Navajo Code Talkers* • *The History of Communication* **WEEK 2** • *A New Language — Invented by Kids!* • *Dolphin Dinner* **WEEK 3** • *Cooper's Lesson* • *The Museum Book*	**WEEK 1** • *What Are the Five Senses?* • *The Science Behind Sight* • *Animal Senses* • *Who's a Hero?* • *Let's Dance Around the World* • *Seven Natural Wonders* • *Mariana Trench* • *Weird and Wondrous Rocks* • *Saving the Kemp's Ridley Sea Turtle* • *How Can Photos Take Us Back in Time?* • *A Tale of Traditional Tales* • *To Your Health!* • *How Technology Has Changed Communication* • *The History of Communication* • *Dolphin Dinner* **WEEK 2** • *The Beatles Were Fab (and They Were Funny)* • *Seeds of Change* **WEEK 3** • *Never Give Up!* • *Why Art Centers Matter* • *Eco-Friendly Food* • *Bug Bites* • *How Can We Reduce Household Waste?*	**WEEK 1** • *The Year of the Rat* • *Now You're Cooking!* • *Luz Sees the Light* • *On Sea Turtle Patrol* • *Cooper's Lesson* **WEEK 2** • *Kitoto the Mighty* • *Catch Me If You Can* • *Prince Charming Misplaces His Bride* • *Perseus and the Fall of Medusa* • *Thunder Rose* • *A Pair of Tricksters* • *In the Days of King Adobe / En los días del Rey Adobín* • *Ten Suns (a Chinese legend); The Ten Suns* **WEEK 3** • *The Game of Silence* • *Rent Party Jazz*
Expository Essay	**Persuasive Essay**	**Biographical Essay**

Get Into Reading!

Grades 3, 4, and 5 of *Into Reading* and *¡Arriba la lectura!* are each organized into 12 modules. Students build knowledge as they read about, write about, view, and discuss each module topic.

¡Arriba la Lectura! cuenta con todo esto y más. En la sección ¡Viva el español! verá lo que distingue a este programa.

GRADE 5 Overview	① Inventors at Work	② What a Story	③ Natural Disasters
❓ **ESSENTIAL QUESTION**	What kinds of circumstances push people to create new inventions?	How does genre affect the way a story is told?	How can learning about natural disasters make us safer?
MODULE FOCUS	🌱 **SCIENCE:** Innovation	📖 **LANGUAGE ARTS:** Story Elements	🌱 **SCIENCE:** Natural Disasters
⚙️ **LEARNING MINDSET**	Trying Again	Wonder	Seeking Challenges
TEXT SETS	**WEEK 1** • Morning Miracles • Government Must Fund Inventors • A High Quality Inventor • Train Talk • The Inventor's Secret **WEEK 2** • Winds of Hope • Wheelchair Sports: Hang Glider to Wheeler-Dealer **WEEK 3** • Captain Arsenio • Girls Think of Everything	**WEEK 1** • Lena and the Lonely Peony: A Story Told in Three Genres • Many Ways to Tell a Story • From Mouth to Page • The Gift of a Story • Airborn **WEEK 2** • The Secret Garden • The Miracle of Spring **WEEK 3** • The Poem That Will Not End • The Mesmer Menace	**WEEK 1** • Nature's Dark Side • Who Studies Natural Disasters? • Help Is on the Way • Eruption! **WEEK 2** • Between the Glacier and the Sea: The Alaska Earthquake • Quaking Earth, Racing Waves **WEEK 3** • Hurricanes • Green City
⬇️ **WRITING FORM**	Expository Essay	Story	Persuasive Essay

4 Wild West	**5** Project Earth	**6** Art for Everyone
What character traits were needed in people who settled the West?	How can caring for Earth and its living things improve life now and in the future?	How do different art forms impact people in different ways?
🌐 SOCIAL STUDIES: Westward Expansion	🌱 SCIENCE: Conservation	🌐 SOCIAL STUDIES: The Arts
Grit	Setting Goals	Belonging

WEEK 1
- *Life in the Wild West*
- *Why Go West?*
- *Houses of Dirt*
- *Explore the Wild West!*

WEEK 2
- *The Celestials' Railroad*
- *Homesteading*

WEEK 3
- *A Pioneer Sampler: The Daily Life of a Pioneer Family in 1840*
- *Along the Santa Fe Trail*

WEEK 1
- *Planet Home*
- *The Protective Power of Nature Preserves*
- *Tech-Trash Tragedy*
- *Potatoes on Rooftops*

WEEK 2
- *Living Green*
- *The Good Garden*

WEEK 3
- *Parrots Over Puerto Rico*
- *The Elephant Keeper*

WEEK 1
- *The World Around Us*
- *Let's Get Creative*
- *Andy Warhol and Georgia O'Keeffe*
- *Christo and Jeanne-Claude*

WEEK 2
- *Rita Moreno*
- *Play, Louis, Play!*

WEEK 3
- *Phillis's Big Test*
- *Miss Alaineus*

Letter	Editorial	Personal Narrative

GRADE 5 Overview (cont.)	⑦ **Above, Below, and Beyond**	⑧ **A New Home**	⑨ **Unexpected, Unexplained**
? ESSENTIAL QUESTION	What role does curiosity play in exploration?	How do people adapt to new experiences and make a new place home?	What makes something mysterious, and what drives people to solve mysteries?
MODULE FOCUS	🌱 **SCIENCE:** Exploration and Discovery	🌐 **SOCIAL STUDIES:** Cultures	🌱 **SCIENCE:** Unsolved Mysteries
⚙ LEARNING MINDSET	Questioning	Growth Mindset	Problem Solving
TEXT SETS	**WEEK 1** • A Hero's Journey • A Few Who Dared • Miss Mitchell's Eclipses • Into the Unknown: Above and Below **WEEK 2** • Great Discoveries • SpaceShipOne **WEEK 3** • The Mighty Mars Rovers • The Day-Glo Brothers	**WEEK 1** • New Kid in Town • Moving to a New Country: A Survival Guide • Liberty Enlightening the World • ⊚ A Movie in My Pillow / Una Pelicula en mi Almohada **WEEK 2** • From Scratch • ⊚ Elisa's Diary / Diario de Elisa **WEEK 3** • Inside Out and Back Again • Love That Dog	**WEEK 1** • What Was That? • Why People Love Mysteries • Searching for Atlantis • Mr. Linden's Library **WEEK 2** • The Loch Ness Monster • Finding Bigfoot **WEEK 3** • The Secret Keepers • The Egypt Game
WRITING FORM	Research Report	Lyric Poem	Imaginative Story

10	11	12
The Lives of Animals	**Genre Study: Nonfiction**	**Genre Study: Literary Texts**
What can we learn about ourselves by observing and interacting with animals?	What are the characteristics of informational text, narrative nonfiction, and persuasive text?	What are the characteristics of realistic fiction, play, and mystery?
SCIENCE: Animal Behaviors	WEEK 1 Informational Text WEEK 2 Narrative Nonfiction WEEK 3 Persuasive Text	WEEK 1 Realistic Fiction WEEK 2 Play WEEK 3 Mystery
Noticing	**Self-Reflection**	**Resilience**

WEEK 1
- *We Are Animals*
- *Why We Watch Animals*
- *Prairie Dogs: Talk of the Town*
- *Willie B.*

WEEK 2
- *Dolphin Parenting*
- *Can We Be Friends?*

WEEK 3
- *Winter Bees*
- *The One and Only Ivan*

WEEK 1
- *Wheelchair Sports: Hang Glider to Wheeler-Dealer*
- *Quaking Earth, Racing Waves*
- *Hurricanes*
- *Christo and Jeanne-Claude*
- *Finding Bigfoot*
- *Can We Be Friends?*

WEEK 2
- *The Inventor's Secret*
- *Winds of Hope*
- *Eruption!*
- *Parrots Over Puerto Rico*
- *The Mighty Mars Rovers*
- *Willie B.*

WEEK 3
- *Government Must Fund Inventors*
- *Potatoes On Rooftops*

WEEK 1
- *The Good Garden*
- *From Scratch*
- *Elisa's Diary / Diario de Elisa*

WEEK 2
- *The Miracle of Spring*
- *Living Green*

WEEK 3
- *Mr. Linden's Library*
- *The Secret Keepers*

Letter to the Editor	**Realistic Story**	**Narrative Poem**

Instructional Model: A Day of *Into Reading*

Target students' diverse needs using whole-class instruction, teacher-led small groups, and options for building independence.

¡Arriba la Lectura! cuenta con todo esto y más. En la sección ¡Viva el español! verá lo que distingue a este programa.

WHOLE-CLASS INSTRUCTION

BUILD KNOWLEDGE AND LANGUAGE/ VOCABULARY	10–15 minutes/day
READING WORKSHOP	20–30 minutes/day
FOUNDATIONAL SKILLS*/ COMMUNICATION	15–30 minutes/day
WRITING WORKSHOP	30–45 minutes/day

** Use flexible grouping to teach **Foundational Skills** lessons based on students' needs.*

WHOLE-CLASS WRAP-UP AND SHARE

5 minutes/day

INDEPENDENT PRACTICE

COLLABORATIVE WORK

45–60 minutes

TEACHER-LED SMALL GROUPS

OPTIONS FOR SMALL GROUPS

TEACHER-LED SMALL GROUPS

GUIDED READING GROUPS

SKILL AND STRATEGY INSTRUCTION

ENGLISH LEARNER SUPPORT

OPTIONS FOR INDEPENDENT AND COLLABORATIVE WORK

LITERACY CENTERS

 READING CENTER

 VOCABULARY CENTER

 DIGITAL STATION

 WRITING CENTER

PROJECT CENTER

myBOOK

Individuals and partners can read and respond to texts.

GENRE STUDY BOOK CLUBS

Students can have meaningful conversations about texts.

STUDENT CHOICE LIBRARY BOOKS

Selecting books for independent reading increases engagement and provides opportunites for students to practice skills and strategies.

INQUIRY AND RESEARCH PROJECTS

Students work on the week's focus for the module project.

Planning for the Year

Follow this suggested timeline to plan instruction and administer assessments throughout the course of the school year.

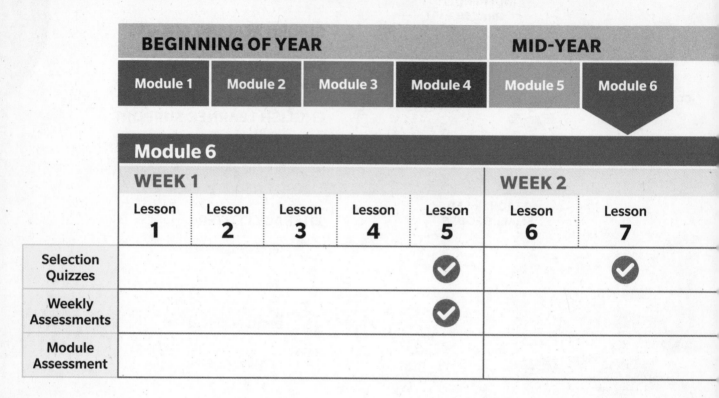

	BEGINNING OF YEAR				MID-YEAR	
	Module 1	Module 2	Module 3	Module 4	Module 5	Module 6

Module 6

	WEEK 1					WEEK 2	
	Lesson 1	Lesson 2	Lesson 3	Lesson 4	Lesson 5	Lesson 6	Lesson 7
Selection Quizzes					✓		✓
Weekly Assessments					✓		
Module Assessment							

Reading Workshop

LESSON SEQUENCE

Build Knowledge and Language

END OF YEAR

| Module 7 | Module 8 | Module 9 | Module 10 | Module 11 | Module 12 |

WEEK 3

Lesson 8	Lesson 9	Lesson 10	Lesson 11	Lesson 12	Lesson 13	Lesson 14	Lesson 15
		✓				✓	
		✓				✓	
							✓

Writing Workshop

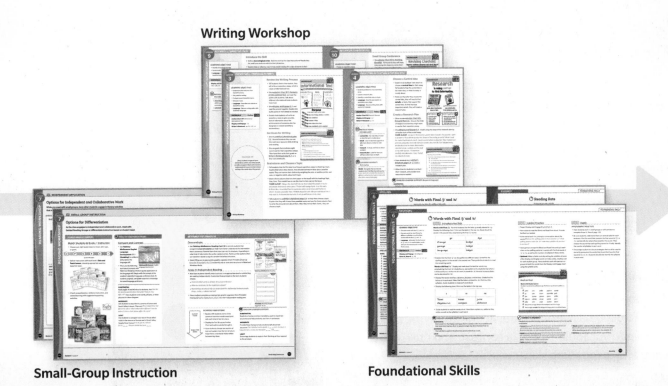

Small-Group Instruction

Foundational Skills

Materials to Build Knowledge and Language

Support students as they build knowledge about topics and genres through collaborative discussion, topic word study, building knowledge maps, and actively viewing and responding.

¡Arriba la Lectura! cuenta con todo esto y más. En la sección ¡Viva el español! verá lo que distingue a este programa.

Teacher's Guide, Volumes 1–5

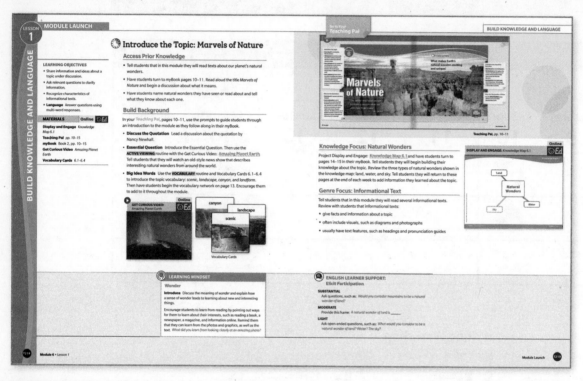

Build Knowledge and Language instruction includes:

- **Introduce the Topic** Students access prior knowledge and build background for content-area and social-emotional topics.

- **Big Idea Words** Across the module, students build Vocabulary Networks based on topic vocabulary and use newly acquired words in their speaking and writing.

- **Knowledge Focus** Students add topic information each week to build complete Knowledge Maps by the end of the module.

Get Curious Videos

Students watch a Get Curious Video at the beginning of each module to build background knowledge about the topic, hear topic-related vocabulary used in context, and build active viewing and responding skills.

Teaching Pal, Books 1–2

At the beginning of each module, students are introduced to the module topic, essential question, and a thought-provoking quotation to help build background for the topic.

Each module's Big Idea Words are introduced through a Vocabulary Network that students can add to throughout the module. A Knowledge Map gives students the opportunity to record their learning about the module topic.

Students revisit these pages at the end of each module to synthesize their knowledge, make meaningful connections, and discuss what they have learned.

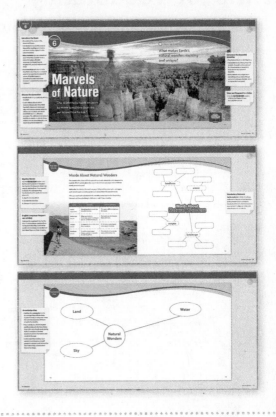

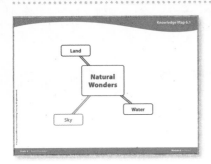

Online Ed Display and Engage: Knowledge Maps

As students read, view, and interact with module texts and activities, they build new knowledge networks. Use the Knowledge Map to preview what students can expect to learn at the beginning of each module. Revisit and add to it each week, and use it to help students synthesize topic information at the end of the module.

Online Ed Vocabulary Cards

Use the Vocabulary Cards to introduce the Big Idea Words to help students understand the words' meanings and connect them to the topic.

Materials for Vocabulary

Support students in acquiring academic vocabulary and encourage curiosity about language.

¡Arriba la Lectura!
cuenta con todo esto y más.
En la sección ¡Viva el español!
verá lo que distingue a
este programa.

Teacher's Guide, Volumes 1–5

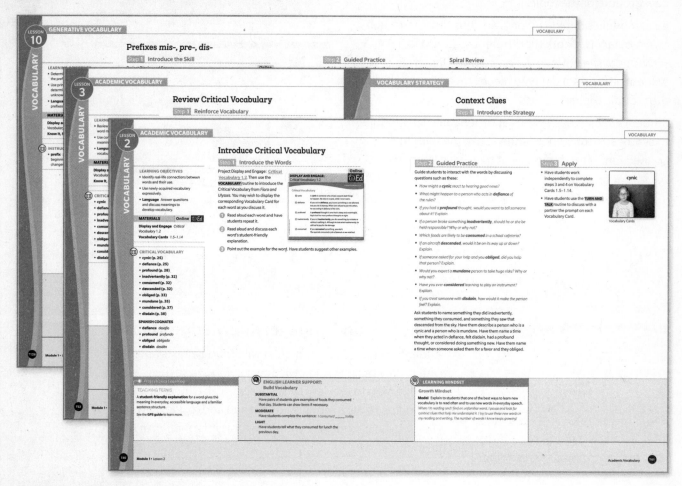

Vocabulary instruction includes:

- **Critical Vocabulary** lessons introduce and review high-utility academic and content vocabulary from students' *myBook* texts.

- **Generative Vocabulary** lessons provide weekly opportunities to use known words as springboards to new, unknown words with morphological or semantic relationships. A Spiral Review within each lesson reinforces prior skills.

- **Vocabulary Strategy** lessons equip students with tools to uncover the meanings of unknown words as they read.

- **Synthesize Knowledge** lessons at the end of each module have students revisit the Vocabulary Networks they have been building from the first day and use the words in different contexts.

Vocabulary Cards

Use the Vocabulary Cards to introduce the module's Critical Vocabulary words from the *my*Book texts.

The front of each card displays the vocabulary word and an image that depicts it. The back of each card guides students to read the word, its meaning, and its use in context, as well as to use the word in a sentence and find words related to it. Students also participate in collaborative discussion to answer questions about the word.

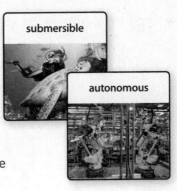

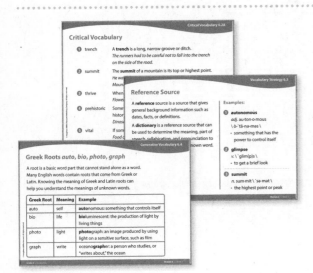

Online ⊙Ed Display and Engage

Project Display and Engage resources for the whole class during Critical Vocabulary, Vocabulary Strategy, and Generative Vocabulary lessons. These digital tools provide visual support to the introduction of the content in each lesson.

Know It, Show It

Students use the Know It, Show It to independently practice using the Critical Vocabulary words and applying the vocabulary skills they have learned each week.

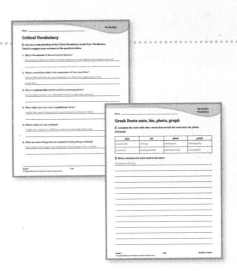

Materials for Reading Workshop

Support students' reading comprehension development through meaningful experiences with texts and opportunities to practice and apply new skills every week.

¡Arriba la Lectura!
cuenta con todo esto y más.
En la sección ¡Viva el español!
verá lo que distingue a
este programa.

Teacher's Guide, Volumes 1-6

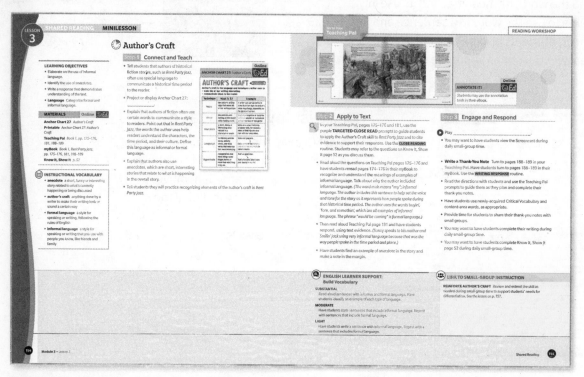

- **Shared Reading** minilessons provide comprehension skill and strategy instruction with application to the student *my*Book texts. Questions and prompts in the Teaching Pal give students opportunities to develop and strengthen close reading skills.

- **Instructional Vocabulary** terms and definitions reinforce students' understanding of and facility with key academic vocabulary.

- **Engage and Respond** activities provide independent practice opportunities for students to respond to the texts in a variety of ways and to cite text evidence in their spoken and written responses.

Anchor Charts

Display the Reading Anchor Charts to support instruction and "anchor" students' learning about comprehension strategies, literary and informational text comprehension skills, and genres. Anchor Charts are also available online as printable resources.

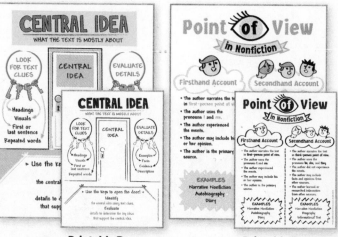

Printable Resource   **Printable Resource**

Genre Study Teacher's Guide

Use the instruction in the Genre Study Teacher's Guide to focus on a literary or informational genre each week. Comprehension skills are viewed through the lens of genre to help students understand the choices authors make to best deliver their messages through a text. Students also examine the impact those choices have on the reader.

myBook, Books 1-2

Ten collections of high-interest, diverse texts in a wide variety of genres are arranged in topically-related text sets for shared or independent reading. The interactive format allows students to annotate the text and take notes directly in their books.

Teaching Pal, Books 1–2

The Teaching Pal provides color-coded, point-of-use instructional notes, prompts, and questions to be used in conjunction with the myBook texts for different purposes over multiple readings:

- Blue **READ FOR UNDERSTANDING** notes are used for a first reading of the complete text to get the gist.

- Purple **TARGETED CLOSE READ** notes are used for close reading and analysis of select sections of the text.

- Red **NOTICE & NOTE** notes are used to alert students to particular signposts in the texts that will help them enhance their understanding.

- Yellow **ACADEMIC DISCUSSION** and other notes are used for pre- and post-reading instructional support.

Know It, Show It

Students independently practice applying comprehension skills to myBook texts.

Materials for Foundational Skills

Support students in building a strong foundation for literacy as they engage in activities that develop and practice decoding, spelling, and fluency skills.

¡Arriba la Lectura! cuenta con todo esto y más. En la sección ¡Viva el español! verá lo que distingue a este programa.

Teacher's Guide, Volumes 1–6

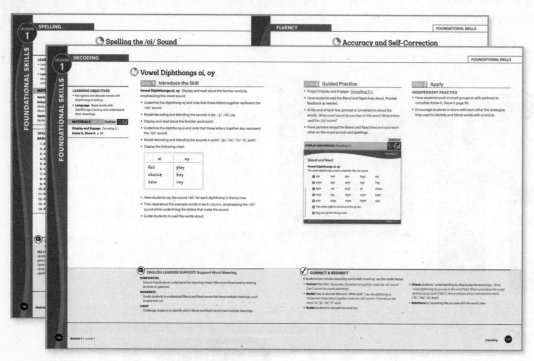

Weekly Foundational Skills instruction includes these elements:

- **Decoding** lessons build on the instruction in earlier grades and help students develop facility with structural analysis in order to read longer words.

- **Spelling** lessons help students make decoding-encoding connections and provide practice for handwriting and keyboarding skills.

- **Fluency** lessons give practice in fluent reading with appropriate rate, intonation, phrasing, expression, and self-correction using context and decoding.

- **High-Frequency Word** cards provide practice in recognizing, reading, and spelling high-utility words.

⌨Ed Display and Engage

Project **Display and Engage** resources for the whole class to practice blending and reading increasingly difficult words and sentences that contain the decoding elements.

Blend and Read

Vowel Diphthongs oi, oy
The vowel diphthongs oi and oy stand for the /oi/ sound.

❶ toil	boil	join	boys	soil
❷ poise	joys	spoil	toys	Troy
❸ joint	coil	broil	oil	choice
❹ hoist	soy	voice	coins	point
❺ joist	ploys	moist	foiled	void

❻ The snake coiled its tail around the oil can.

❼ Roy put soil into his toy truck.

Know It, Show It

Students independently practice and apply what they have learned in the decoding lessons.

⌨Ed Printable Resources

Access online **Printable Resources** to provide additional practice with fluency skills each week.

Materials for Communication

Support students in strengthening their speaking and listening skills and building and practicing their research and media literacy skills.

¡**Arriba la Lectura!**
cuenta con todo esto y más.
En la sección ¡Viva el español!
verá lo que distingue a
este programa.

Teacher's Guide, Volumes 1–5

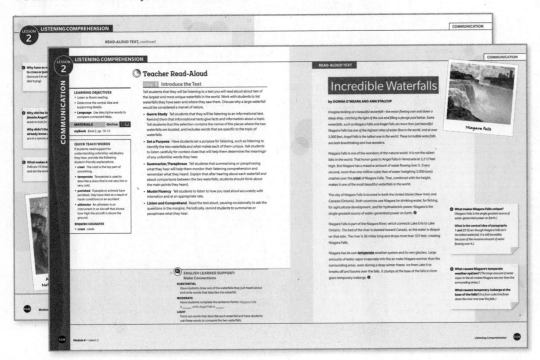

Weekly Communication instruction includes:

- **Listening Comprehension** lessons with a Teacher Read-Aloud to model fluency, monitor listening comprehension, and build background for the module topic.

- **Research and Media Literacy** and **Speaking and Listening** lessons help students develop, build, and strengthen critical oral and written communications skills.

- **Making Connections** lessons at the end of every module give students the opportunity to communicate what they have learned through their synthesis of topic knowledge across the module.

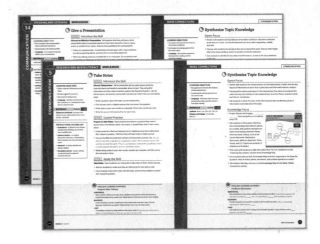

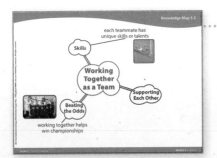

Display and Engage

Project **Display and Engage** resources for the whole class to supplement the core instruction with visual examples.

Materials for Writing Workshop

Build students' writing independence through interactive writing and process-based lessons that strengthen their developing skills.

¡Arriba la Lectura! cuenta con todo esto y más. En la sección ¡Viva el español! verá lo que distingue a este programa.

Writing Workshop Teacher's Guide

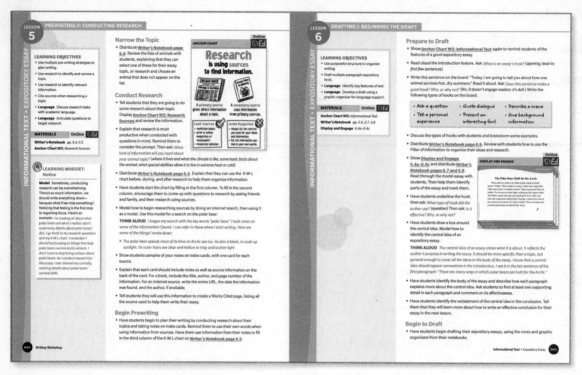

Writing Workshop instruction includes:

- Modules that explore **genre characteristics** of narrative, informational, argument, correspondence, and poetry writing.

- Authentic **connections between reading and writing** using mentor texts.

- **Interactive writing** to support developing writing skills and daily opportunities for **independent writing.**

- **Process-based writing** to generate ideas, organize drafts, revise and edit, and publish.

- Minilessons for ideas, organization, word choice, conventions, and presentation that follow a **gradual-release model.**

- Support for **peer feedback and conferences** to provide guidance with revising and editing writing.

- **Embedded grammar lessons** within the writing instruction, along with a bank of grammar minilessons for direct instruction on specific grammar topics.

Writer's Notebook

Students use the **Writer's Notebook** for direct support as they plan, organize, and revise their writing. Students record interesting words and phrases to use in their writing, set goals, choose and narrow topics, interact with a student model, and plan their writing with graphic organizers.

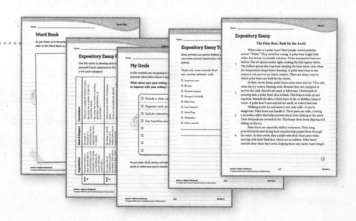

⊙Ed Anchor Charts

Display the Anchor Charts or use them as models to create your own charts to "anchor" students' learning about features of writing forms, craft and structure, and grammar and conventions.

Anchor charts are also available online as printable resources for students to keep and reference in their writing folders.

Writing Anchor Charts in Grade 3

- Task, Audience, and Purpose
- Research Sources
- Elements of a Narrative
- Crafting Dialogue
- Elements of Informational Text
- Elements of an Argument
- The Central Idea
- Elements of Poetry

- Parts of a Formal Letter
- Revising Checklist
- Editing Checklist
- Improving Word Choice
- Capitalization Rules
- Punctuation Marks
- Proofreading Marks
- Publishing Options

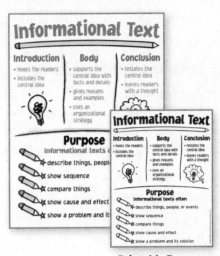

Printable Resource

Additional Writing Anchor Charts in Grades 4 and 5

- Asking Questions
- Elements of a Personal Narrative
- Narrative Structure

- Types of Conflict
- 5+1 Ways to Start a Story
- Elements of Descriptive Writing
- Elements of Research

- Elements of Figurative Language
- Tips on How to Present

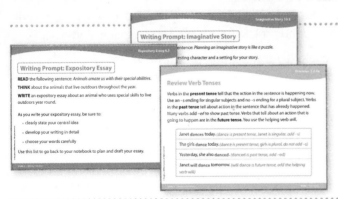

⊙Ed Display and Engage

Projectable **Display and Engage** resources include writing prompts, student models, grammar support, and revising and editing checklists.

⊙Ed Printable Resources

Access **Writing Graphic Organizers** online to provide independent practice with planning, organizing, and drafting a variety of writing types.

- Story Map
- Two-Column Chart
- Three-Column Chart
- Four-Column Chart
- Idea-Support Map

- Web
- Time Order Chart
- Story Structure
- Problem Resolution Chart

- Inference Map
- Central Idea Map
- Four-Square Map
- Flow Chart
- Feature Map

Use **Reproducible Rubrics** to review students' writing in conferences and throughout the writing process to foster improvement.

Materials for Guided Reading

Support students in building knowledge and reading independence by using leveled texts during small-group guided reading.

Rigby Leveled Reader Library

Use Rigby Leveled Readers and Leveled Reading Cards to match students to texts based on guided reading level, skill, topic, genre, or interest. Each grade offers a continuum of 90 fiction and informational texts.

GRADE 3

Levels L through Q, 15 titles per level

GRADE 4

Levels O through T, 15 titles per level

GRADE 5

Levels R through W, 15 titles per level

📶 Take and Teach Lessons

Each Rigby Leveled Reader and Leveled Reading Card has a corresponding Take and Teach Lesson that includes:

* Text X-Ray and text complexity measures.
* flexible use sessions that allow teachers to select text and instruction based on genre, target skill, or topic.
* coordinated instructional segments with stopping points to ask guided questions.
* scaffolding for English learners.
* a bank of student response activity options that support and reinforce comprehension.

📶 Leveled Reader Quizzes

Assess students' comprehension of each Leveled Reader with a quick comprehension quiz, available as a printable resource for a pencil-and-paper test or used as a digital auto-scanned assessment.

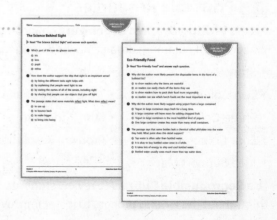

Materials to Support English Learners

Meet with English learners to target their language development and provide support at various proficiencies.

Teacher's Guide, Volumes 1-5

Daily small-group lessons in the Teacher's Guide provide additional support for English learners and focus on a particular language function for the week. Use the text-based prompts in the lessons to guide students' application of the language function.

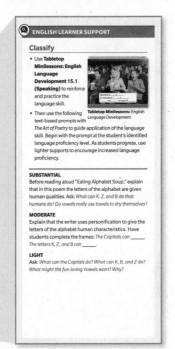

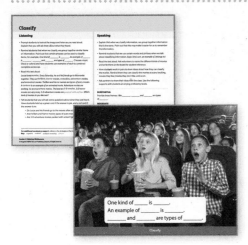

Tabletop Minilessons: English Language Development

Use the minilessons to provide instruction for each week's language function, with a different daily focus on one of these domains:

- Listening
- Speaking
- Reading
- Writing
- Collaborative Problem-Solving

Online Ed Printables

Students can use the Language Graphic Organizers to guide their interactions with texts they read independently and apply the weekly language function.

Materials to Reinforce Skills and Strategies

Provide targeted support for skills and strategies introduced during whole-group minilessons.

¡Arriba la Lectura! cuenta con todo esto y más. En la sección ¡Viva el español! verá lo que distingue a este programa.

Teacher's Guide, Volumes 1–5

Daily small-group lessons in the Teacher's Guide reinforce and extend comprehension skill and strategy instruction from the shared reading minilessons.

- Review the whole-group minilesson skill with students in small groups, based on need.
- Guide students to apply the skill to self-selected books for independent reading.
- Use the Scaffold and Extend notes and the English Learner Support to tailor instruction based on the needs of the students in each group.

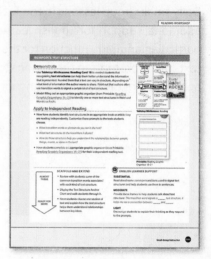

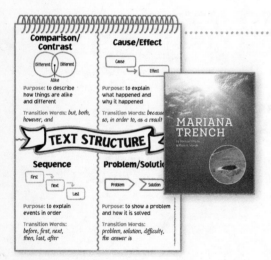

Tabletop Minilessons: Reading

- **Instruction** for key reading skills and strategies in a small-group setting
- **Student-facing Anchor Charts** on stand-up charts with teacher support on the back
- **Differentiated** skill instruction that can be used with any text

Online ⊙Ed Printables

Students can use the Reading Graphic Organizer printables to guide their interactions with the texts.

Materials for Literacy Centers

Introduce Literacy Centers to students working independently and with partners while you meet with students in small groups.

¡Arriba la Lectura! cuenta con todo esto y más. En la sección ¡Viva el español! verá lo que distingue a este programa.

Teacher's Guide, Volumes 1–5

The Teacher's Guide includes weekly ideas for Literacy Centers that reinforce and extend what students are learning through direct instruction.

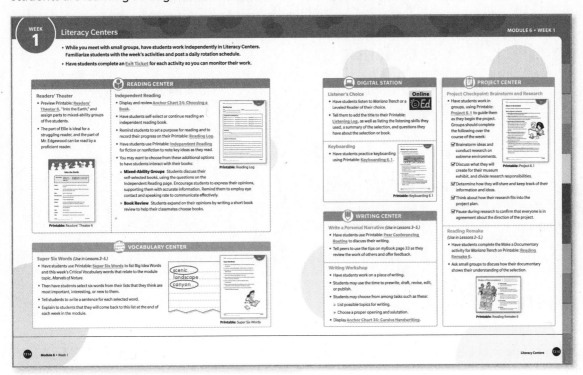

Reading Center

 Students use the **Reading Log** printable to track their independent reading progress and reflect on it throughout the year. They also work collaboratively in mixed-ability groups to read aloud the topic-based **Readers' Theater** scripts with fluency and expression.

Vocabulary Center

 Students use the **Super Six Words** printable to further explore module vocabulary they found important and interesting.

Digital Station

 Students use the **Listening Log** printable to demonstrate active listening skills and listening comprehension and the **Keyboarding** printables to practice keyboarding skills.

Writing Center

 Students work independently on the Writing Workshop assignment for the week. They also use the **Peer Conferencing Routine** printable to discuss their writing with peers.

Project Center

 Reading Remake printables develop students' reading response skills through a variety of engaging formats.

- Write a News Story
- Make an Invention
- Make an Infographic
- Make Field Guide
- Make a Flipbook
- Make a Documentary
- Make a Mural
- Make a Book Trailer
- Make a Trading Card
- Write a Poem

Assessments

Use assessments to track students' progress and determine when they need extra support or practice.

¡Arriba la Lectura! cuenta con todo esto y más. En la sección ¡Viva el español! verá lo que distingue a este programa.

Online Ed Intervention Assessments

Administer the **Screening Assessment** to screen and diagnose students for intervention instruction, determine flexible groups for foundational skills instruction, and monitor progress as needed.

ASSESSMENT TYPE	FREQUENCY	SKILLS ASSESSED
Screening	• Beginning of year	• Oral Reading Fluency
Diagnostic	• Follow-up, as needed	• Print Concepts Inventory • Phonological Awareness Inventory • Letter-Sound Correspondences
Progress Monitoring	• Every two weeks, as needed	• Oral Reading Fluency

Online Ed Weekly and Module Assessments

- Weekly Assessments: 1 per week; 36 total
- Module Assessments: 1 per module; 12 total

Administer the paper-and-pencil or online **weekly and module assessments** to assess:

- reading comprehension
- vocabulary strategies
- generative vocabulary
- grammar
- writing (module)

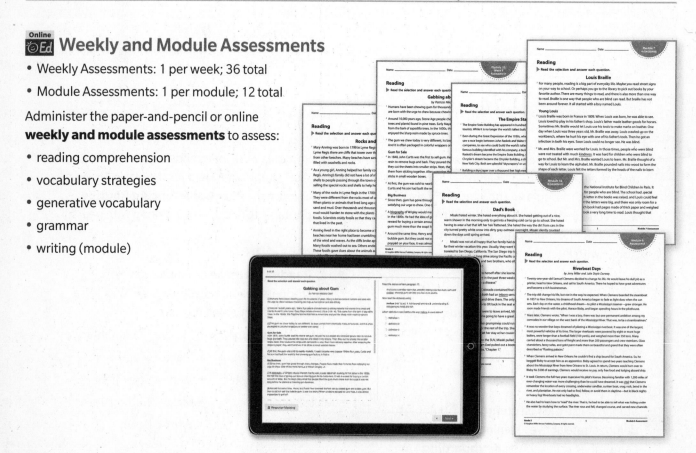

Selection Quizzes

- 1 per main *my*Book text; 40 total

Administer the paper-and-pencil or online **Selection Quizzes** to assess comprehension of the main selections.

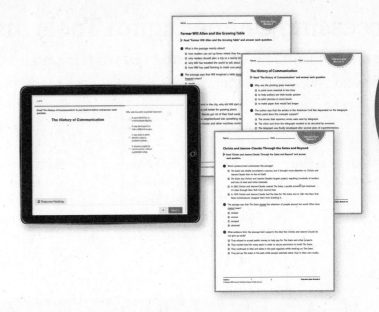

Data Reports

View **data reports** online to analyze students' gaps and gains, group students for differentiated instruction, and locate resources to target students' learning needs.

- Assessment Report
- Single Assessment Drilldown
- Standards Report

Rubrics

Use the following online rubrics available to assess students' writing and projects:

- Narrative Writing
- Informational Writing
- Poetry Writing
- Correspondence Writing
- Argument Writing
- Collaborative Discussion
- Response Writing
- Inquiry and Research Project

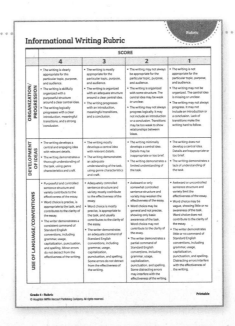

See pages 78–91 for more information about Grades 3–5 assessments, data, and reporting.

WELCOME TO *INTO READING*

Accessing Online Digital Tools and Resources

Use the online management center "Ed: Your Friend in Learning" to plan and teach lessons, analyze student data, and access teaching and professional learning resources.

DISCOVER Browse Resources by category, such as Teacher's Guide.

CREATE Customize your teaching plans and assessments to match district requirements or to meet students' needs.

DATA & REPORTS Use reports to track students' progress and identify areas for differentiated instruction.

WELCOME Select **Roster** to set up your class and add students.

MODULES Click a module to access teacher and student materials for each lesson.

RESOURCES View resources for teaching lessons, assessing students, differentiating instruction, communicating with families, and accessing professional learning information.

STANDARDS Locate resources correlated to your standards or use the search tool to search by key word.

GROUPS Create and manage groups based on your own classroom observations and assessment results.

Modules

Access a digital version of the Teaching Pal.

View the resources available for the entire module.

Find the *my*Book selection titles for each week.

View the digital resources available for each lesson, including the Teacher's Guide lessons.

Teacher's Guide and Teaching Pal

Choose a resource category to **browse**, such as Teacher's Guide.

Use the **Table of Contents** filter to choose a specific module, week, or lesson.

Filter resources by **Instructional Purpose**, **Audience, Lexile,** or **Guided Reading Level.**

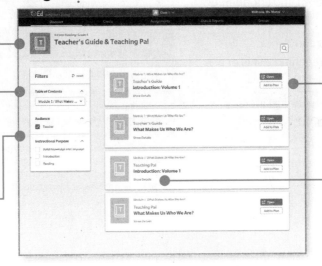

Open the resource, assign it to students, or select **Add to Plan** to customize your teaching plans.

Choose **Show Details** to read a description of the resource.

Data and Assessments

Find the percentage of students at different levels of proficiency using the **Assessment Proficiency** graph.

Track students' **Assessment Performance** to more effectively differentiate instruction.

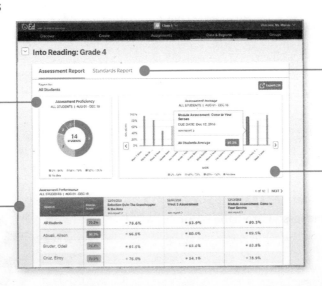

Use the **Standards Report** to follow students' progress in standards proficiency and to access resources that support student learning.

Evaluate the average class score for each assessment with the **Assessment Average** graph.

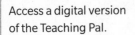

Building Expertise with Connected Professional Learning

Engage in ongoing professional learning through embedded teacher support, facilitated sessions, and coaching.

Embedded Support

The Teacher's Guide includes embedded support for building professional knowledge and for enhancing your instruction with high-impact strategies.

On the Spot Professional Learning

Look for blue boxes in the Teacher's Guide Volumes for research-based support at the beginning of the year. Support is offered for these categories:

- **Getting Started** notes provide implementation support for introducing classroom and engagement routines.
- **Research Foundations** notes convey research-based rationales for teaching a skill or a particular instructional approach.
- **Teaching Terms** notes define technical literacy terms and clarify commonly confused terms, using examples.
- **Best Practices** notes offer research-based suggestions for effective teaching.

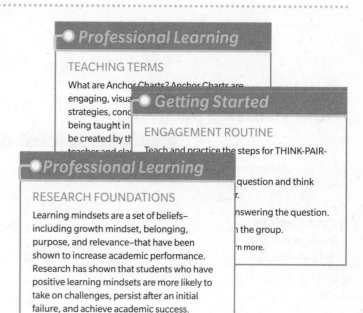

Professional Learning

TEACHING TERMS

What are Anchor Charts? Anchor Charts are engaging, visua... strategies, conc... being taught in... be created by th... teacher and cla...

Getting Started

ENGAGEMENT ROUTINE

Teach and practice the steps for THINK-PAIR-... ...question and think ...r. ...nswering the question. ...h the group. ...n more.

Professional Learning

RESEARCH FOUNDATIONS

Learning mindsets are a set of beliefs–including growth mindset, belonging, purpose, and relevance–that have been shown to increase academic performance. Research has shown that students who have positive learning mindsets are more likely to take on challenges, persist after an initial failure, and achieve academic success.

TEACHER TIP

Continue to use the Vocabulary Cards throughout the year to review words from previous lessons. With repeated exposure, students will find it easier to use the words in everyday conversation and in their writing.

Teacher Tips

Use the orangeTeacher Tip feature in all modules of the Teacher's Guide to give you easy-to-implement suggestions for adapting or extending instruction to practice and apply skills.

Online ⓔ Ed Classroom Videos

View online videos that show teachers in classrooms modeling a range of instructional routines and lessons from the program.

Personalized Blended Professional Learning

Explore ongoing, comprehensive support for implementing *Into Reading* and
¡Arriba la Lectura! and for further developing effective teaching practices.

Getting Started with *Into Reading*

Attend professional learning sessions in-person or online. Topics include:

- Experiencing *Into Reading*
- Using resources for planning and teaching
- Accessing student and teacher technology
- Administering assessments and using data

The interactive **Professional Learning Guide** supports the
Getting Started sessions and provides practical information
for implementation.

Online ⓔEd On-Demand Getting Started Modules

Explore a series of interactive digital topics designed to provide
immediate support for getting started. You can view these topics
sequentially when you begin teaching *Into Reading* and decide which
ones to revisit for a refresher.

Follow-Up Support

Choose from a variety of topics, such as whole- and small-group
routines and lessons, data and reports, or assessment and
differentiation, to design an in-person or live online experience to meet your goals.

Coaching

Grow in your understanding of how to use *Into Reading* to support
student achievement through blended coaching from an HMH
consultant on topics such as instruction, lesson design, data-driven
decision making, and more.

askHMH

Get on-demand access to program experts who will answer questions
and provide personalized conferences to support implementation.

Ongoing Support

Work with HMH consultants to develop instructional practices that cultivate strong
readers, writers, and critical thinkers.

Learn more at **https://professionalservices.hmhco.com/**.

Arranging the Classroom

Organize your classroom environment with areas for whole-class instruction, small-group time, and Literacy Centers.

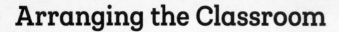

READING CENTER 📖

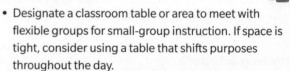

WHOLE GROUP 👥

- Arrange desks for the whole class in a way that enables students to easily see the screen or whiteboard without obstruction.

- Individual desks should be grouped in a way that allows students to work in teams or pairs during whole-group work.

- Use wall space around the community area to display the calendar, messages, and other important content.

SMALL GROUPS 👥

- Designate a classroom table or area to meet with flexible groups for small-group instruction. If space is tight, consider using a table that shifts purposes throughout the day.

- Choose an area away from more collaborative work spaces to help students in the group focus.

- Store materials such as Leveled Readers, Tabletop Minilessons, and instructional cards nearby. Provide space for a laptop or tablet for teacher access to digital resources and support.

DIGITAL STATION

WRITING CENTER

VOCABULARY CENTER

PROJECT CENTER

LITERACY CENTERS

- Provide multiple places in the classroom where students can engage in Literacy Center work, such as for the Writing Center, Project Center, and Digital Station.

- Provide designated areas with materials and resources students need to complete tasks independently and in pairs or groups.

- Designate a comfortable space in the classroom for a Reading Center so students can enjoy quiet independent reading time.

For additional information about setting up Literacy Centers, see pages 44–47.

Classroom Considerations

Consider these suggestions for setting up a student-friendly learning environment:

- Anticipate traffic flow at different times of day to determine placement of furniture and other objects.

- Set up systems of expectations and routines to maintain an organized classroom and limit clutter.

- Resist overcrowding the room and allow students to co-create the space throughout the year.

- Provide multiple areas in the classroom for students to collaborate or work independently.

- Make available flexible seating, such as sensory seats, stools, or bean bag chairs.

- Consider using neutral colors for the overall scheme and brighter, stimulating colors only as accents.

- Create a warm environment by making use of natural light and lamps when possible.

- Designate a quiet space where students can go when they need to regulate strong emotions.

Creating a Literacy-Rich Environment

Build a literacy-rich environment and a community of learners in which every student is a reader and a writer.

¡Arriba la Lectura! cuenta con todo esto y más. En la sección ¡Viva el español! verá lo que distingue a este programa.

Building Vocabulary

Since words are the basis of listening, speaking, reading, and writing, students who enter school with more words are at an advantage. To help close this gap and to provide a literacy-rich environment, there must be numerous opportunities—both formal and informal—for students to grow their vocabularies in service of learning and socializing. Teachers cannot directly teach the estimated thousands of words necessary to "do school," so the classroom environment needs to be rich in print and send the message that words matter.

Make It Personal

Work together to create a classroom that reflects the students in your class and conveys a message that everyone has a space. Personalize the classroom using students' names, photos, and interests.

- Survey students in order to offer books that match their reading interests.

- Designate a wall space or other visible area to post students' writing.

- Have students begin on a wall, chart paper, or poster board a vocabulary network based on those in their *my*Book and have them add to and curate it throughout the school year.

TEACHER ↔ TO TEACHER
From the Classroom

❝ *We talk about and practice the expectations for working in centers a lot during the first few weeks of school. It makes all the difference when I start meeting with my small groups.* ❞

Getting Started with Literacy Centers

Well-defined and organized Literacy Centers provide students with opportunities to practice skills, make decisions, and work cooperatively. Guidance is provided in the Teacher's Guide at the beginning of each week. Most Literacy Center activities require specific printables, noted in the Teacher's Guide.

Reading Center

In the Reading Center, students build reading skills, stamina, and enjoyment by self-selecting books for independent reading, discussing texts with classmates, and participating in readers' theater activities.

How to Prepare

- Designate a quiet area of the classroom with easy-to-browse bookshelves and a seating area for students to read independently and to discuss their reading with peers.

- Offer books in a variety of genres, topics, reading levels, and formats, being sure to include books based on students' interests. This may also be a place to house student-made books.

- Include pencils, markers, and copies of the Reading Log, Reading Literature, and Reading Nonfiction printables.

Vocabulary Center

In the Vocabulary Center, students practice using the Big Idea Words and Critical Vocabulary Words.

How to Prepare

- Laminate the Super Six Words printable and place it in the center.

- Stock the center with paper, pens, and pencils.

- Students will need to retain their lists for each of the three weeks of a module. You may wish to provide a place in the Vocabulary Center for students to keep their papers for easy access.

Digital Station

At the Digital Station, students can participate in activities such as practicing their keyboarding skills and reading along as they listen to the *my*Book texts.

How to Prepare

- Set up a designated table near electrical outlets for several desktop computers and keyboards, tablets, and headphones so that students can work without disturbing others.

- Post log-in information, as needed, as well as a list of the programs or apps students can use while they are at the Digital Station.

- Remind students to treat the equipment with care, keep tablets and laptops charged, and know whom to contact if a technical issue arises.

- Keep copies of the Listening Log Printable and the Keyboarding Printables available for student use.

Writing Center

In the Writing Center, students work on their written responses to the *my*Book texts as well as on their Writing Workshop assignments.

How to Prepare

- You may wish to post information about the assignments and due dates, as well as a copy of *my*Book bookmarked for the current response-writing activity.

- Stock the center with paper, pens, and pencils for students to draft or finalize their papers.

- Provide access to computers and a sign-up sheet with time limits if students need to take turns.

- Provide a copy of the rubrics for Writing Workshop assignments.

 Project Center

In the Project Center, students work each week on one segment of the Inquiry and Research Project and on the Reading Remake activity for the module. Over the course of the module, students collaborate to generate ideas, conduct research, finalize, and present an inquiry-based project.

How to Prepare

- Provide the Project printable for each week and the Reading Remake printable for the module. You may wish to laminate the Reading Remake printables.

- Gather and set out the materials needed for each stage of the Inquiry and Research Project and for the Reading Remake. Check that students understand the overall project goals, and each step they need to complete.

- Give students options for organizing their research questions and project work from week to week so they can readily pick up where they left off each time they visit the Project Center.

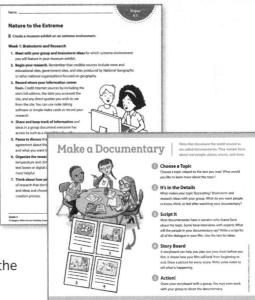

Scheduling for Success

Use these suggestions to help you plan an *Into Reading* schedule that suits your needs.

¡Arriba la Lectura!
cuenta con todo esto y más.
En la sección ¡Viva el español!
verá lo que distingue a
este programa.

Sample Schedules

Following a consistent schedule helps students know what to expect and helps you make the most of instructional time. Consider these recommendations for how much time to spend on each *Into Reading* section, and use the sample schedule as a jumping-off point for creating your own plan.

VOCABULARY	10–15 minutes
READING WORKSHOP	60–85 minutes
FOUNDATIONAL SKILLS *or* COMMUNICATION	15–30 minutes
WRITING WORKSHOP	30–45 minutes

ACTIVITY	TIME
Greet Students + Announcements	10 minutes
Vocabulary	15 minutes
Reading Workshop	15 minutes
Guided Reading + Small Groups/ Independent Reading + Literacy Centers	70 minutes
Lunch	20 minutes
Recess	30 minutes
Foundational Skills *or* Communication	30 minutes
Writing Workshop	45 minutes
Math	45 minutes
P.E./Art/Music	30 minutes
Science/Social Studies	30 minutes
Wrap-Up	10 minutes

Best Practices for Scheduling

No two classrooms are the same, so it's crucial to consider students' needs, your own preferences, and school requirements when scheduling. Here are some tips for planning a day that works for you.

- Incorporate choice into the day where possible. Allowing students some freedom to choose how to spend certain periods of time gives them a sense of agency and instills decision-making skills.

- Be realistic about how long students are able to attend well to any activity. Include "body breaks" and "brain breaks" throughout the day, particularly for longer stretches. Getting students moving and giving them time to blow off steam helps them get the most out of instructional time.

- Create shorter instructional segments, as needed, especially at the beginning of the year. Provide quick breaks between these segments during which students can choose to read independently, work on a group project, or catch up on work. Mixing it up keeps students engaged.

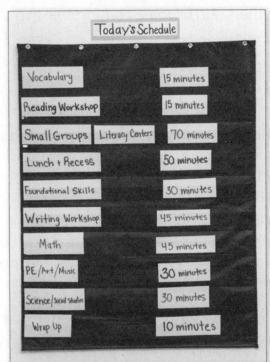

Today's Schedule	
Vocabulary	15 minutes
Reading Workshop	15 minutes
Small Groups / Literacy Centers	70 minutes
Lunch + Recess	50 minutes
Foundational Skills	30 minutes
Writing Workshop	45 minutes
Math	45 minutes
P.E./Art/Music	30 minutes
Science/Social Studies	30 minutes
Wrap Up	10 minutes

TEACHER ⟷ TO TEACHER

From the Classroom

❝ *Scheduling is everything. Kids thrive on a regular schedule, but the day also needs to be dynamic, to keep them engaged. Once I figured out how to tailor my schedule to the needs of the classroom, my instruction really took off.* ❞

Welcoming Students to School

Set the tone for the year with carefully planned opportunities for students to meet others and become comfortable in the classroom during the first days of school.

Meeting and Greeting

Use the first few days of school to help students build a sense of community.

- **After welcoming students to the classroom, start with an activity.** Let students settle in with a quiet activity that reinforces the idea of each student belonging to the class community. For example, have students decorate a name tag, make labels for supply bins, or make a self-portrait to post.

- **Introduce.** Use morning meeting time to introduce students to their peers. Have each student pair up with someone they do not know well. Give partners time to find out three things about each other. Then have the students introduce each other to the rest of the class by sharing those three things.

Getting Familiar with the Classroom Environment

Familiarizing students with the classroom environment during the first few days of school promotes comfort and creates excitement, giving students a sense of ownership over their space and providing opportunities to model expectations.

- **Point out the zones in the classroom.** Introduce students to different areas of the classroom, such as the Reading Center, Vocabulary Center, Digital Station, Writing Center, and Project Center. Encourage students to ask questions about the centers and about other zones in the room.

- **Introduce flexible work areas.** Explain to students that they can use these areas to work in groups of different sizes and for different purposes. Create a system of expectations and routines for work in small groups and at the Literacy Centers.

- **Share location of materials.** Show students where to find basic materials, such as writing materials, reading materials, and art materials. Emphasize the importance of sharing these items and replacing them after each use.

- **Build social skills.** Tell students they will be responsible for caring for shared spaces and supplies as well as helping out when they see a need.

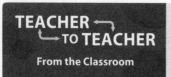
TEACHER → TEACHER
From the Classroom

> 66 *After a guided discovery, I like to do an interactive writing activity. This helps reinforce what children learned and it gets them to work together as a team—building a sense of community right away.* 99

Setting Goals with Students

Have students set goals to give them a sense of purpose and to motivate them to take on new challenges.

Establish Goals

As students become more familiar with the objectives and expectations for their grade levels, lead them to articulate specific and achievable learning goals for the year.

I will use three new words each week in my writing.

- **Clarify.** Explain that setting goals will help students make progress each week.

- **Set.** Prompt students with questions about some of the topics for the year, such as *What do you hope to learn about this topic?* Model setting goals, such as *I will read two books each week. I will use three new words each week in my writing.* Tell students they will record their own goals for each week. Encourage students to set goals that are measurable and achievable.

- **Brainstorm steps.** Discuss with students a few ways to reach their goals. For example, if one goal is to use the week's vocabulary words in both speaking and writing, students can agree to practice using a couple of the words each day.

- **Track.** Tell students to record their goals in their journals and to revisit them often to track progress and reflect on their learning.

Measure Reading and Writing Goals

Before beginning each module, review Kicking Off the Module! in the Teacher's Guide for goal-setting suggestions. Have students revisit and refine their goals as they progress through the module.

Work with students to adjust expectations and make a plan to reach each goal as needed. Help students articulate, track, and revisit specific goals during reading and writing conferences and guide them to adjust their plans as needed.

Celebrate Success

When students reach a goal, celebrate it! You may wish to create rewards to acknowledge and celebrate success. Possibilities include:

- No Homework Pass
- Extended Center Time
- Leading a Class Activity
- Lunch with the Teacher

Establishing Classroom Routines

Clear and consistent classroom routines help all students follow expectations, focus on productive learning, and build confidence and independence.

Classroom Management Routines at a Glance

You may want to consider establishing some or all of the classroom management routines at the beginning of the year.

CLASSROOM MANAGEMENT ROUTINES
• Quiet Cue
• Silent Signals
• Active Listening
• Ask Three, Then Me
• Partner Up

It's All Routine!

The time and effort you spend introducing and practicing routines during the first weeks of school will set the tone for the whole school year.

• **Ask for input.** Students are more likely to feel invested in following routines if they help create them.

• **Keep steps simple and positive.** As you record routines, try to reframe negative language. For example, use "Walk slowly" instead of "No running" or "Listen carefully" instead of "Don't talk."

• **Make it visual.** Post the steps for important routines in appropriate areas.

• **Be explicit.** Teach students the steps of each routine and model expectations with examples and non-examples. Then provide opportunities for students to practice.

• **Problem-solve as a class.** If you notice a breakdown in a routine, bring students together to share your observations, review the routine, and talk through solutions.

● Professional Learning

RESEARCH FOUNDATIONS

❝ *By explicitly teaching routines to students, teachers can (a) set students up for success, (b) decrease the possibility of behavior errors, and (c) reduce the amount of time spent reminding students about the routines on a daily basis.* ❞

—Myers et al. (2017)

QUIET CUE

QUIET CUE is a clear, consistent, and quick routine to cue students to stop what they are doing and listen for directions.

Use this routine:

- while students are working in small groups or independently.
- at the start of a transition from one activity to the next.

IMPLEMENTATION SUPPORT

- Choose an audible signal, such as chimes or a rain stick, a clapping pattern, or a verbal cue.
- Demonstrate the quiet cue and model expectations for students to stop what they are doing, to look, and to listen.
- Make sure to wait until all students are looking and listening before giving directions.

SILENT SIGNALS

SILENT SIGNALS are a set of nonverbal hand signs that students can use to get your attention without interrupting a lesson.

Use this routine:

- during whole-class lessons.
- when you are working with small groups or individuals.
- during classroom transition times.

IMPLEMENTATION SUPPORT

- Identify the most frequent reasons students may need to get your attention. Assign a simple hand sign for each need, or work with the class to decide on signals.
- Explain the purpose of using silent signals and introduce signals like these: crossed fingers for using the restroom, three fingers in a "w" shape for water, and raising a hand for help. Add signals as a group as different needs arise.
- Practice as a class; for example, say "restroom" and have students use the signal. Make sure that students know how you will respond to each signal.

GIVE ME FIVE

GIVE ME FIVE is a routine that teaches the elements of active and respectful listening.

Use this routine:

- before beginning a whole-group lesson or activity.

- when students are sharing ideas or presenting writing to the class.

- to prepare students for a classroom visitor.

IMPLEMENTATION SUPPORT

- Explicitly teach, model, and practice the elements of active listening at the beginning of the school year.

- Explain that students can prepare to listen actively by focusing themselves physically and mentally:

  » *Keep your eyes and ears focused on the speaker. Bring your attention back to the speaker if you are momentarily distracted by other sights and sounds.*

  » *Avoid excessive movement that distracts you or others.*

  » *Avoid talking to other listeners or interrupting the speaker.*

  » *Keep an open mind. You might not agree with everything a speaker says but listen actively in order to understand the speaker's points.*

- Maintain reasonable expectations for still bodies and be aware of students who may be better listeners while moving or fidgeting. In these cases, consider using stress balls or flexible seating, such as cushioned seats.

- Use the following checklist to evaluate students' mastery of this active listening routine:

  ☐ Did the student look at the speaker, instead of looking around the room or looking at others?

  ☐ Did the student refrain from interrupting or talking to others while the speaker was speaking?

  ☐ Did the student remain relatively still and avoid excessive movement?

  ☐ Did the student ask questions or make comments after the speaker finished that indicated comprehension of the speaker?

ASK THREE, THEN ME

ASK THREE, THEN ME is a strategy to minimize interruptions by encouraging students to ask three classmates a question before coming to you with the question.

Use this routine:

- when you are working with a small group.

- during Writing Workshop or other times when students are working independently and you are conferring with others.

IMPLEMENTATION SUPPORT

- Ensure that students working independently have clear procedures for their tasks and easy access to the materials they need.

- Describe the types of information students can request from other students before coming to you, such as the location of a resource or basic task details.

- If a student comes to you before asking three classmates for help, remind the student of the routine.

- During the whole-group wrap-up, ask students to reflect on how well they used "Ask Three, Then Me." Work through any problems together.

PARTNER UP

PARTNER UP is a strategy for pairing students to collaborate as partners.

Use this routine:

- before partner discussions.

- to kick off partner reading.

- when students are working on projects or doing other work with partners.

IMPLEMENTATION SUPPORT

- Before pairing students, pay special attention to students' English proficiency and ability to stay on task.

- Assign a number (1 or 2) to each partner. Ask students to confirm their number by raising a hand when you call their number.

- Tell students which partner goes first. *Number 1 partners share first this time. Number 2 partners listen. Then switch.*

- If you have an odd number of students, assign one pair to have an additional Number 2 partner. Both Number 2 partners share when it is their turn.

- Partner students for a set amount of time, and change partners frequently—for example, every two weeks.

Creating a Culturally Responsive Environment

¡Arriba la Lectura! cuenta con todo esto y más. En la sección ¡Viva el español! verá lo que distingue a este programa.

Cultivating a classroom where every student feels welcomed, appreciated, and encouraged is a process that spans a teacher's entire career. Whether you're just starting to actively promote inclusivity and resist bias in the classroom or have spent a lifetime doing so, consider these suggestions for helping create a culturally responsive, anti-bias environment for your students.

Don't Avoid Differences—Embrace Them

It's wonderful to teach students the ways in which we're all the same. In fact, to some teachers it may seem misguided to talk about differences at all. But pointing out how we're unique (judiciously and respectfully) demonstrates to students that our differences are to be celebrated, not glossed over. Strive for a balance between pointing out ways we're alike and ways we're unique.

Honor Home Languages

It's increasingly common for students to speak a language other than English at home. Creating links between students' home languages and the English-learning environment at school is key to fostering a sense of belonging for students.

A simple way to do this is to ask students to share a few words or phrases in their home languages, and have the class learn them. As a teacher, you can take it upon yourself to learn a few more words, and share those. You'll be showing students that you respect their home languages and that you, too, are a language learner!

Show a Variety of *Good* Representations

An essential part of making students feel validated and affirmed is exposing them to books and other learning materials that reflect who they are in terms of ethnicity, culture, family structure, or socioeconomic status.

While having a good *quantity* of varied representations is important, it's not the same as *quality*. Some "diverse" books actually reinforce stereotypes and bias. It's important to show students that doctors, executives, farmers, artists, and people in all professions come from a wide range of backgrounds. Seek out materials that reject stereotypes and reflect the limitless possibilities of all students.

The texts featured in *Into Reading* were carefully chosen with this philosophy in mind. Extend this approach to other materials you bring into the classroom, ensuring that all students see themselves reflected and are shown possibilities for lives that move beyond the ones they know best.

Learn about Cultural Differences

As a teacher, stay mindful of the fact that certain ways of behaving can have different meanings in different cultures. This applies not only to interactions with students, but also to interactions with their families. For example, you may have a student whose parents were born in Mexico. When the parents visit school, they decline to come inside the classroom. To some teachers, that might seem indicative of disinterest. In fact, it's the opposite—in their home culture, classrooms are sacred spaces where only teachers and students tread!

Be Mindful of Gender Considerations

As students grow their vocabularies, they're exposed to messages that the subtleties of language can send. It's best if students learn the gender-neutral versions of common words. Think "businessperson" instead of "businessman," "firefighter" instead of "fireman," and so on. ("Fire*fighter*" sounds cooler anyway!)

Point Out Bias

When an instance of bias *does* arise—in perhaps an older book or between students at recess—seize the opportunity for a teachable moment. Point out why the instance of bias is wrong and hurtful, and you'll be helping students learn to be more aware of bias themselves.

○ Professional Learning

RESEARCH FOUNDATIONS

❝ *When children see themselves and their families reflected in their early childhood setting, they feel affirmed and that they belong. When children's identities and families are invisible, the opposite happens. Children feel that they are unimportant and do not belong.* ❞

— Derman-Sparks and Olsen Edwards (2009)

Social-Emotional Learning

Helping students build a strong social-emotional foundation can lead to school success and a lifetime of benefits.

Lead with a Learning Mindset

A **learning mindset** is a set of beliefs that drives students to seek challenges, feel that school is a safe place to make mistakes, and know that there is value in working hard. Set students up for success by introducing and reinforcing each of these beliefs throughout the year.

Growth Mindset: *the belief that people can increase their ability*

Individuals with a growth mindset believe that intelligence and ability can be developed through hard work, while those with a fixed mindset believe they are born with a set amount of effort and learning. Students with a growth mindset are more likely to pursue challenges and persist through them because they believe they are capable of improving.

Help students establish a growth mindset by explicitly teaching these key ideas:

- Focused effort and practice are more important than talent when working to master a new skill.

- Mistakes, challenges, and setbacks are all essential parts of the learning process.

- The connections in your brain grow and change with effort and practice—the more you use it, the stronger it becomes.

● *Professional Learning*

RESEARCH FOUNDATIONS

66 *Mindset is not a fixed attribute. Like other beliefs, it is learned from experience and instruction. Intervention studies show that students' motivation, perseverance and achievement can be increased by teaching a growth mindset.* 99

—Dockterman & Blackwell (2014)

Purpose and Relevance: *the belief that work has value*

Students are more likely to value their daily work when they understand its purpose and relevance to their own goals or interests.

Help students see the value of their daily work by guiding them to answer:

• Why am I doing this?

• How will this task help me in the future?

See GPS, page 51 to learn more about setting goals with students.

Belonging: *the belief that one is part of an academic community*

When students feel a sense of belonging, they are more likely to take academic risks, ask for help, and try new things.

See GPS, page 63 to learn about tips for establishing a sense of belonging in your classroom.

Professional Learning

RESEARCH FOUNDATIONS

> *The feedback teachers give students can influence their mindsets in surprising ways . . . [A study found that] when students were praised for having high ability, they came to attribute their success to a fixed (and unchangeable) quality of themselves, while students praised for effort believed that their performance was subject to improvement.*
>
> — MindsetWorks®

Learning Mindset: Grades 3–5

Into Reading and *¡Arriba la Lectura!* incorporate the latest research from Mindset Works®
and from Dr. David Dockterman of Harvard's Graduate School of Education. Students
focus on one learning mindset behavior or skill per module that is closely connected to
the module topic and reinforces a specific learning mindset belief.

BEHAVIOR/ STRATEGY	LEARNING MINDSET BELIEF			KEY MESSAGES
	Growth Mindset	Belonging	Relevance/ Purpose	
seeking challenges	⚙			*Seeking challenges, trying new things, and not being afraid to fail is an important part of learning!*
belonging		⚙	⚙	*You are valuable members of our learning community—we are all here to help each other learn and grow.*
curiosity	⚙		⚙	*Curiosity leads to learning—when you ask questions and explore new ideas your brain grows.*
asking for help	⚙	⚙		*Asking for help is one way of "trying smarter." Learning from others can help you get unstuck and help you go further.*
problem solving	⚙			*There are many different ways to solve a problem—looking for clues, asking for help, trying a different way.*
grit	⚙		⚙	*As you persist in learning new things, you can discover ways to apply what you learned.*
purpose	⚙		⚙	*The work you do in school and in life has a purpose.*
noticing	⚙		⚙	*Paying attention to details helps you learn new things, and it helps you improve your work.*
resilience	⚙		⚙	*Our brains are like muscles—the more we use them, the stronger they get. Hard work and our response to failure along the way lead to learning.*
setting goals	⚙		⚙	*You can achieve your goals by making a plan and persisting through challenges.*
perseverance/ trying again	⚙			*When you persevere through a problem by trying new strategies, the neurons in your brain form new connections. That makes your brain stronger and smarter!*
self-reflection	⚙		⚙	*Good learners reflect on their work and effort by asking themselves, "How can I make this better? How will this help me accomplish my goal(s)?"*
planning ahead	⚙			*Setting goals and planning steps we can take to meet our goals helps us reach those goals one step at a time.*
growth mindset				*Our ability grows with our effort. The harder we work, the smarter we become.*
wonder				*Reflecting on our work and making connections to our interest and goals make us better learners.*
questioning				*Asking questions is about being open to new ideas and trying new things.*

GRADE 3 MODULE	GRADE 4 MODULE	GRADE 5 MODULE
2. Use Your Words	3. Rise to the Occasion	3. Natural Disasters
1. What a Character!	5. Art Everywhere	6. Art for Everyone
	11: Genre Study: Nonfiction	
5. Teamwork		
8. Imagine! Invent!	10. Communication Nation	9. Unexpected, Unexplained
3. Let Freedom Ring!	9. Global Guardians	4. Wild West
7. Make a Difference		
6. Animal Behaviors	2. Come to Your Senses	10. The Lives of Animals
12. Genre Study: Literary Text	4. Heroic Feats	12: Genre Study: Literary Texts
		5. Project Earth
10. Tell a Tale	12: Genre Study: Literary Texts	1. Inventors at Work
4. Stories on Stage	7. Tricksters and Tall Tales	11: Genre Study: Nonfiction
9. From Farm to Table	8. Food for Thought	
11. Genre Study: Nonfiction	1. What Makes Us Who We Are?	8. A New Home
	6. Marvels of Nature	2. What a Story
		7. Above, Below, and Beyond

Social-Emotional Learning

Teaching Learning Mindset Skills

As students move through the module, use the learning mindset resources to introduce the learning mindset focus and lead students to apply it and reflect on it.

Introduce and define the learning focus using the My Learning Mindset Anchor Chart and the model language in the Teacher's Guide.

Apply the learning mindset focus in the context of daily lessons using the strategies in the Learning Mindset notes in the Teacher's Guide.

Reflect on the learning mindset focus at the end of each module and reinforce key concepts. For example, recognize when students apply the mindset focus and acknowledge their learning.

Reinforce Learning Mindset

Develop an awareness of your own mindsets, and infuse learning mindset behaviors into teaching and learning throughout the year.

- **Be mindful.** Consider how your own mindsets crop up in your language and teaching practices.

- **Praise effort instead of intelligence.** Instead of saying *"You're so smart,"* try, *"I noticed that you were frustrated when you didn't get the answer the first time, but you tried it again and you figured out the problem. Good job!"*

- **Normalize frustration.** Help students understand that struggling with a challenging task is common and productive. *"No one does everything right the first time they do something new. What's important is that you keep trying."*

- **Communicate with families.** Send home the Family Letter printable for each module to help families understand the learning mindset focus students are working to develop and encourage them to reinforce it at home.

- **Celebrate learning mindset.** Acknowledge students for their hard work in developing learning mindset behaviors.

My Learning Mindset
Ways of thinking that help me learn and succeed

Asking for Help	Belonging	Grit
I ask questions when I get stuck.	I help my classmates. My classmates help me.	Hard work leads to success.
Noticing	**Perseverance**	**Planning Ahead**
I look closely.	I learn from my mistakes.	What steps can I take to reach my goals?
Problem Solving	**Purpose**	**Resilience**
I try different ways to solve problems.	How can this help me outside of class?	I won't give up. I will keep trying.
Seeking Challenges	**Self-Reflection**	**Growth Mindset**
I like to try things that seem difficult.	How can I make this even better?	The harder I work the stronger I become.

LEARNING MINDSET

Challenge Yourself

Apply Remind students to think about learning new words. Encourage them to find ways to use the new words in their own conversations and writing. *Try giving yourself "points" for using a new word outside of class. You can think about and take satisfaction using the word, or you can actually "keep score" in your no...*

LEARNING MINDSET

Seeking Challenges

Reflect Encourage students to think about the people who faced the Galveston hurricane in 1900. *When you face a big challenge, you succeed if you do not give up. You face the challenge step by step until it is over.*

Building Students' Sense of Belonging

Establishing a sense of belonging—the belief that everyone is respected and valued—is central to creating a learning environment where all students thrive.

Belonging is the belief that one is respected and valued. Students who feel they belong in their school environment are likely to be engaged, resilient learners.

Create Community

Early in the year, use these strategies to establish a sense of community.

- **Make students feel welcome.** Help students get to know one another and celebrate the individual experiences each student brings to the classroom.

- **Co-create expectations.** Work with students to create expectations, routines, and procedures to give them a sense of control and to make them feel valued.

- **Consider the physical environment.** Allow students to feel a part of the classroom community by keeping the walls empty at the beginning of the year and having students work together to create and decorate their space.

- **Connect with families.** Send home a welcome letter to introduce yourself to families, share information about how they can get involved at school, and encourage them to connect with one another to build a support system for students that extends beyond school.

Strengthen Connections

Reinforce students' sense of belonging throughout the year.

- **Use images and texts.** Thoughtfully display images that represent the diversity of your class, select books and media that are relevant to all students, and display photos of students' communities and families.

- **Connect daily.** Make an effort to recognize and connect with each student daily. For example, greet students individually at the beginning of the day. Throughout the day, acknowledge students by making eye contact and by using their names when addressing them.

- **Build in collaboration time.** Establish routines that encourage peers to share equally, such as the **THINK-PAIR-SHARE** and **TURN AND TALK**.

- **Teach social skills.** Hold regular class meetings to model social skills, including how to handle conflicts that may arise.

- **Involve families.** Encourage family participation in school events and activities whenever possible.

Social-Emotional Learning

Promoting Positive Behavior

Set positive behavior goals that require students to meet the expectations in different classroom contexts and school settings.

Establish Expectations

Use the examples below as a guide for establishing clear behavior expectations during different times of the day. Post them in the classroom.

	WHOLE-GROUP INSTRUCTION	SMALL-GROUP INSTRUCTION	LITERACY CENTERS/ INDEPENDENT WORK
Be Respectful	• Listen with your whole body—eyes, ears, and heart. • Stay in your seat. • Use kind words.	• Listen with your whole body—eyes, ears, and heart. • Keep your hands and feet to yourself.	• Use a quiet voice. • Work collaboratively with others. • Share materials.
Be Responsible	• Follow the teacher's directions. • Take care of books and materials.	• Follow the teacher's directions. • Go to the small-group table quickly and quietly.	• Come prepared to participate. • Take care of books and materials. • Put away materials before moving to a new center.
Do Your Best	• Participate in every lesson. • Speak loudly enough and clearly when you share.	• Participate in every lesson. • Complete work neatly.	• Help your group or partner. • Complete work neatly.

Support Positive Behaviors

Program materials can be used to remind students of positive behaviors and reinforce positive communication habits in the classroom.

Anchor Charts

• How to Have a Discussion

• Ask and Answer Questions

• Following and Giving Instructions

Teacher's Guides

Use lessons in the Teacher's Guides to teach and reinforce good communication habits.

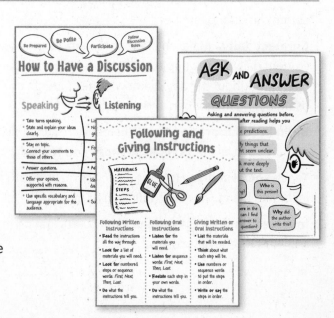

Best Practices: Reinforcing Positive Behavior

Keep in mind these key points for promoting positive behavior in your classroom.

- **Teach and model expectations.** Start teaching classroom expectations and procedures on the first day of school. Model examples and non-examples for each behavior and give students opportunities to practice and role-play. Consider having students co-create the rules and expectations for class to promote student agency and a sense of belonging.

- **Give behavior-specific feedback.** For example, instead of saying *"Good job!"* try *"You were very responsible when you put away all the materials. Thank you!"*

- **Use positive language.** For example, use *"Be respectful"* instead of *"Don't be rude"* and *"Use a quiet voice"* instead of *"Don't yell."*

- **Consider room arrangement.** Ensure that furniture placement promotes smooth transitions from one activity to the next and allows you ready access to a student when a nonverbal reminder of expectations is warranted. Offer strategic seating choices to students, making sure that students with behavior challenges sit near you and not each other.

- **Create a quiet space.** Designate a place in the classroom for "peace and quiet" where students know they can go when their emotions get in the way of learning. Be clear that this space is not intended for "time out" or seclusion.

- **Acknowledge positive behavior.** "Catch" students in the act of following expectations and acknowledge the behavior. You may want to reward students for positive behavior by allowing them extra time for a favorite activity.

- **Communicate with families.** Share behavioral expectations with families early in the year with a note home and at back-to-school night. Throughout the year, touch base with families and let them know when their students succeed!

Social-Emotional Learning

¡Arriba la Lectura!
cuenta con todo esto y más.
En la sección ¡Viva el español!
verá lo que distingue a
este programa.

Support Social-Emotional Learning with Texts

Social-emotional development is key to students' education. Students develop social-emotional skills as they become more aware of their own feelings and needs as well as the needs and feelings of others. Frequent exposure to books allows students to view others' experiences and emotions through the eyes of the people and characters in each text. In fact, research has shown that students who are read to the most, understand others the most. Books help students analyze relationships, see how others handle problems, and make human connections.

● Professional Learning

BEST PRACTICES

It is not enough to simply teach students to read; we have to give them something worth reading. Something that will stretch their imaginations, something that will help them make sense of their own lives and encourage them to reach out toward people whose lives are quite different from their own.

Make Learning Stick

Books are powerful tools for teaching social-emotional skills because they serve as examples of important behaviors, actions, and emotions. Here are some ways to help students develop social-emotional competencies as they read.

- Use a question to prompt students to respond to social-emotional aspects of the book. *How did the character show kindness? What was the character determined to do? What problem did the character face? How did he/she handle the problem?*

- Point out examples of characters who do and don't show self-regulation, kindness, or empathy. Then model or role-play the situation with students to emphasize social cues and how to discuss their own feelings and behaviors.

- It is likely easier to talk about difficult situations for characters in a book than it is to talk about such situations in students' own lives. Talk about how the people or characters in the book handled a tricky situation. Then ask students if they've ever had a similar experience. Allow them time and space to share.

- Throughout the day, pay attention to how students interact with one another. Comment when you see them helping one another, developing friendships, solving problems together, or when they develop and carry out plans. Connect these observations to texts you've read together.

Build a Social-Emotional Library

Help students develop social-emotional skills by using *Into Reading* literature to support the development of key social-emotional competencies.

SOCIAL-EMOTIONAL COMPETENCY	GRADE 3 TEXTS	GRADE 4 TEXTS	GRADE 5 TEXTS
Self-awareness	*Marisol McDonald Doesn't Match; Judy Moody, Mood Martian; The Upside Down Boy; Rosie Revere, Engineer*	*Yes! We Are Latinos; The Year of the Rat; Kitoto the Mighty; Blind Ambition; My Diary from Here to There; Seeds of Change; Cooper's Lesson*	*The Inventor's Secret; The Poem That Will Not End; Rita Moreno; A Movie in My Pillow; From Scratch; Inside Out and Back Again; Mr. Linden's Library*
Self-management	*Zach Jumps In!; Scaredy Squirrel; The Upside Down Boy; Gigi and the Wishing Ring*	*Flora and Ulysses; Blind Ambition; The Game of Silence; Rent Party Jazz; Catch Me If You Can; Perseus and the Fall of Medusa; Thunder Rose; In the Days of King Adobe*	*The Miracle of Spring; The Good Garden; Rita Moreno; Play, Louis, Play!; Phillis's Big Test; A Movie in My Pillow; Elisa's Diary; Inside Out and Back Again*
Social Awareness	*The U.S. Constitution; Why We Celebrate the Fourth of July; Let's Build a Park; Farmer Will Allen and the Growing Table; One Plastic Bag; Energy Island: How One Community Harnessed the Wind and Changed Their World; The Storyteller's Candle; Great Ideas from Great Parents*	*Smokejumpers to the Rescue!; The Battle of the Alamo; Mariana Trench; Nature's Wonders; Eco-Friendly Food; Luz Sees the Light; On Sea Turtle Patrol; How Can We Reduce Household Waste?; Seeds of Change*	*Airborn; Quaking Earth, Racing Waves; Phillis's Big Test; Elisa's Diary; Inside Out and Back Again; Willie B.*
Responsible Decision-Making	*The Flag Maker; Timeless Thomas: How Thomas Edison Changed Our Lives; One Plastic Bag; Energy Island: How One Community Harnessed the Wind and Changed Their World; The Storyteller's Candle; Great Ideas from Great Parents*	*The Year of the Rat; The Battle of the Alamo; In the Days of King Adobe; Eco-Friendly Food; How Can We Reduce Household Waste? Seeds of Change*	*The Miracle of Spring; Eruption!; A Pioneer Sampler; Living Green; The Good Garden; Christo and Jeanne-Claude; The Mighty Mars Rovers*
Relationship Skills	*Dear Primo: A Letter to My Cousin; Dear Dragon; Teamwork = Victory!; Soccer Shootout; Running Rivals; Brothers at Bat*	*The Year of the Rat; The Game of Silence; Rent Party Jazz; Now You're Cooking; Luz Sees the Light; A New Language — Invented by Kids; Cooper's Lesson*	*Living Green; From Scratch; Elisa's Diary; Can We Be Friends?*

Engaging Families as Learning Partners

Building partnerships with families and engaging them in their children's literacy learning can lead to a lifetime of benefits.

¡Arriba la Lectura! cuenta con todo esto y más. En la sección ¡Viva el español! verá lo que distingue a este programa.

A Culture of Collaboration

When families participate in their child's literacy development, children have improved achievement, better school attendance, and reduced dropout rates (Segal & Martin-Chang, 2018). Begin building home-school literacy partnerships by working to initiate a culture of collaboration with families:

- Communicate early in the year with parents and caregivers so that you can leverage their ongoing support.

- Focus initial communications on accomplishments and positive observations.

- Provide clear paths and options for family engagement that are sensitive to constraints families are experiencing.

- Take into account any local considerations, and collaborate with families to develop a family involvement plan that works for the community.

The Role of Families

One of the most impactful practices is to encourage students' parents and caregivers to think of themselves as educators. In addition to providing opportunities for families to become involved within the school day, you can partner with them to support their children beyond the classroom.

Share key practices with families to support their children's literacy success:

- Inform parents and caregivers of the cumulative effect of missing school, and intervene to support families facing challenges with regular **attendance.**

- Provide strategies for helping children develop their **vocabulary knowledge.**

- Demonstrate interacting with students while **reading together** and by **listening to students read aloud.**

- Send home ideas for **authentic reading and writing opportunities.**

● Professional Learning

BEST PRACTICES

Parents, caretakers, and friends are critical to the learning process. Communication with those at home is essential to building a successful classroom environment. Caretakers should be aware of the topics and skills students are learning about at school. Students should be encouraged to use vocabulary, practice reading skills, and discover new reasons to read at home.

Let's Talk

Through conversations with their children, parents and caregivers help them understand word meanings, sentence structure, and social language. Strong oral language skills and deep vocabulary knowledge are critical for reading success.

Encourage families to support oral language development by:

- Playing word games, telling and writing stories, and discussing texts.
- Having conversations throughout the day—on the way to school, at the grocery store, and during shared meals.
- Modeling social aspects of language such as greeting and introducing people and adding relevant comments to conversations about topics of interest.

Let's Read

When parents and caregivers make shared reading time interactive and meaningful, students become successful and motivated readers. Promote effective strategies for families to read together:

- Demonstrate fluent reading with prosody, expression, and enthusiasm. Show how to interact with children while reading together by demonstrating the types of questions to ask about the text.
- Provide ideas for books to read across genres, both for children's independent reading and for families to read aloud. Reading aloud books two years above children's reading level exposes them to academic vocabulary and more complex syntax and help them improve listening and reading comprehension.

Be a Bookworm

The amount that children read by themselves and with others strongly contributes to how well they read and how much they enjoy reading (Cunningham & Stanowich, 2012). To promote reading volume:

- Ensure that families have access to an abundance of appropriate books during the school year and over the summer.
- Coach parents and caregivers on how to consider children's interests and allow them to select related texts. Let parents know that magazines, graphic novels, and online resources count as reading, too!
- Encourage families to gradually stretch reading sessions over time.

Communicating with Families

Keep families informed of their children's progress, and communicate ways you can work together to meet students' learning needs throughout the year.

A Great Start

For some students, starting a new school year can be both exciting and stressful. The first day of school can also be emotional for students' families.

Consider these suggestions for welcoming new families into the school community:

- Mail a personal letter or postcard to students and let them know you are looking forward to meeting them on the first day of school.

- Call students' parents or caregivers to introduce yourself and answer any questions about the first week of school.

- Make sure to provide translations of any communication or handouts and have translators available for meetings or conferences, if needed.

Meet the Families

Use your time at back-to-school night to meet students' family members and set the tone for the year.

- Let parents know how often they should expect to hear from you and how and when they can reach you.

- Convey your homework policy, making sure to stress the importance of making time for unstructured free time, frequent conversations, reading independently and together, family time, and sleep.

- Display *Into Reading* or *¡Arriba la Lectura!* materials for parents to browse through, and explain the curriculum.

- Inform parents of volunteer opportunities and how they can get involved at school or in the classroom throughout the year.

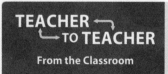
TEACHER ⟵⟶ TO TEACHER
From the Classroom

> 66 *I have each child write a letter or draw a picture for their parents to read at back-to-school night, and I encourage parents to write a letter back to their child. Children are thrilled to find their parents' responses the next day!* 99

Foster Ongoing Outreach

Communicate to families that they can be active participants in their child's learning, and identify specific ways for them to participate. This will help families understand expectations and feel confident about their roles.

- Send home the Family Letter printable at the beginning of each module to inform family members about what their children are learning and to offer practical ideas for reinforcing skills.

- Post family letters and other communications on a board outside or just inside the classroom door.

- Work with other teachers to host family workshops that focus on specific aspects of support for children at home, such as social-emotional learning, shared and independent reading strategies, writing opportunities, and summer learning.

- With appropriate permission, take photos or videos of students and their work to share with parents through text, email, or on a secure class website.

- Invite families to special events where they can view students' projects and watch their presentations!

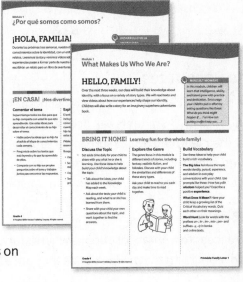

Communicating Progress

Hold conferences with parents or caregivers to share observations about students' development and discuss strategies for working together.

- Start with the positive, focusing on the student's particular strengths or progress since your last meeting or conversation.

- Share the student's reading, writing, and other learning goals.

- Review the student's portfolio with samples of his or her work and classwork that shows growth.

- Share assessment scores and individual reports, making sure to explain where the data come from and what they mean.

- Print a copy of the **Student Growth Report** to discuss the student's Lexile growth.

- Provide specific strategies and resources for parents to support their child's learning outside of school.

- Keep a log to record important notes about parent communications and areas that require follow-up.

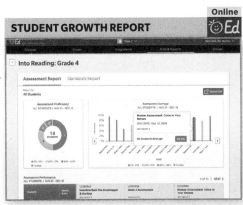

Learning Beyond the Classroom

Provide resources for parents and caregivers to engage in rich and rewarding literacy experiences beyond the classroom.

Online Resources

Provide parents, caregivers, and after-school staff with login information so that students can access online resources to support their learning. Make sure to be sensitive to Internet safety and access issues, working with caregivers to provide resources that work in their personal circumstances.

eBooks

Provide access to a library of eBooks where students can listen to and read along with the *my*Book texts they are using in class.

Printable Resources

Based on students' individual needs, email or provide copies of Printable Resources to parents or caregivers to use outside of school.

Independent Reading

Encourage families to set up a dedicated time at least once per week to read with their children, to listen as their children read aloud to them, and to discuss what they are reading. Send home a copy of the Reading Log printable so that students can record time spent reading outside of class.

Provide simple strategies such as these to support families as their children select a book that is suitable for their reading level:

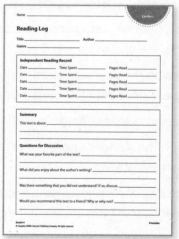

Reading Log

- **Five Words** Children read 2-3 pages of their chosen book and count the words they misread. If they miss five or more, they should choose a less-challenging book. If they don't miss any words, the book is too easy. If they miss 2-3 words, the book is just right for their independent reading level.

- **Book Browse** Children page through the book to see whether it interests them and whether or not they think it looks too difficult or too easy.

Dictation Sentences

Share with family members the Dictation Sentences printables to give students practice at home with the Basic and Review Spelling Words each week.

- Family members may wish to read aloud each boldfaced word and then the context sentence in which it appears. Students can either spell the words orally or in writing.

- Encourage family members to check students' work and provide additional practice for those words with which students struggle.

- Family members may wish to continue with the Challenge Words for students who are ready.

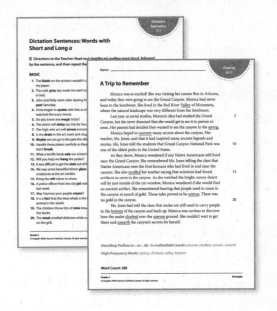

Fluency Passages

Share with family members the weekly Fluency printable. The fiction and nonfiction passages on these printables align with the module topic and include both embedded high-frequency words and words with the week's decoding element, giving students practice with fluent reading.

Provide ideas for using the printables. For example:

- Have a family member read alternate paragraphs or lines of dialogue with the student.

- Have students read the passage through several times until they can read them fluently and with the appropriate expression, rate, and phrasing.

- Encourage family members to note where students stumble and provide additional practice with reading the words, sentences, or paragraphs.

Keyboarding Practice

Support keyboarding skills and practice with the Keyboarding printables.

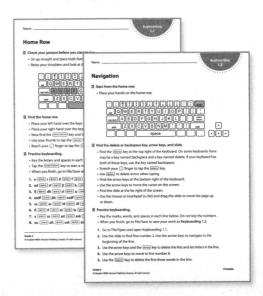

Celebrating Success

Communicate students' successes to their families and celebrate their efforts throughout the year.

Reach Out to Families

Consider students' family members and caregivers when choosing the best strategies for keeping them informed of their children's successes at school.

- During drop-off or pick-up time, make a brief connection to verbally share targeted feedback.

- Designate a board near the classroom to display student writing, projects, or other work for families to view.

- Make a call or send a text, email, or note.

- Share pictures or videos of student work via text, email, or a secure class website, making sure that you have appropriate permissions.

Share Accomplishments

You may want to create certificates and send them home to share students' accomplishments with their families. Possibilities for certificates include:

- Mindset Master

- Remarkable Reader

- Word Wizard

- Wonderful Wordsmith

- Sensational Speller

- Careful Keyboarder

- Proactive Problem-Solver

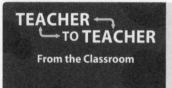
TEACHER ⟶
⟶ TO TEACHER
From the Classroom

❝ *I try to visit each of my students' homes at least once during the school year. It's usually just a quick check-in, but it strengthens my relationship with the entire family and helps me better understand where the child is coming from.* ❞

Supporting Summer Learning

At the end of the school year, offer families strategies and resources to keep their children's minds active during the summer.

Beat the Summer Slide

Give families ideas and resources to support students' literacy over the summer.

- Visit a local library before the school year ends to sign students up for library cards. Have students browse books and learn about summer reading programs. Encourage families to visit the library regularly and continue to read every day.

- Provide a summer reading list with suggestions of titles across a variety of genres for students to read independently and with their families.

- Provide a list of questions to ask students before, during, and after reading.

- Share login information for literacy apps that students can access over the summer.

- Inform families of literacy games they can play together.

Get Out and About

With sensitivity to families' circumstances, suggest accessible experiences and local events that will spark students' interest in topics and ideas they might want to read about, write about, and participate in during the summer months.

- Participate in a book club or other events at the library or a bookstore.

- Grow a garden or cook a family recipe together.

- Create a detailed map of the neighborhood.

- Explore a local park or join a community garden.

- Visit an art or science museum.

- Visit the zoo or an aquarium.

- Attend a concert, play, or other performance students might enjoy.

- Look for announcements from the local library or department of parks and recreation to recommend events and activities in your area.

○ Professional Learning

RESEARCH FOUNDATIONS

66 *During the summer months, young children lose literacy gains made during the school year, a phenomenon known as "summer slide." The most important thing teachers can do to reverse this trend is to help families adopt family literacy routines and promote opportunities for families to talk, read, and write together throughout the school year.* 99

— Hoisington (2017)

Connecting with the Community

Connect students and their families to the larger community to make learning meaningful, teach important skills, and access resources.

Take a Trip

Field trips can bring learning to life and often provide some of the most memorable learning experiences students have during the school year. Remember that field trips don't have to be expensive or logistically challenging. There are often destinations within walking distance that give students opportunities to learn more about the community around them.

To make the most of a field trip:

- prepare by providing student with related books, magazines, and web pages.
- invite parents and caregivers to chaperone, observe their children in a different context, connect with their children's friends and teacher, and learn about community resources.
- take photos during field trips to share on a class website or in a family newsletter.
- reflect with students after the trip by writing about and discussing what they learned.

Invite Classroom Guests

Reach out to students' family members and other community members to share resources or discuss their expertise. For example, the local librarian can visit to tell students about summer reading programs and firefighters can visit to answer students' questions about their careers in fire safety. When logistics make a visit unfeasible, consider setting up a video chat to bring the community to the classroom.

Brainstorm questions to ask guests. When possible, have guests provide a hands-on demonstration of their work for students to experience. Take photos and record information to use as sources for research writing or projects.

Give Back to the Community

Throughout the year, engage students in service projects to develop social awareness, responsibility, and citizenship. For example, students can visit a local preschool to share books with younger children, write cards for a senior center or children's hospital, or participate in a local cleanup effort. Encourage students to generate additional ideas for service projects.

Community Connections

Consider these ideas to plan meaningful experiences with the community beyond school. Whenever possible, engage family members to come in and share experiences, photographs, and other artifacts.

CLASSROOM GUESTS	FIELD TRIPS
School workers, such as a principal, crossing guard, custodian, nurse, or cafeteria worker, can talk about the role they play in the school community.	Visit the classroom of younger children and have students tell them what to expect in their grade level.
Former students who are now in high school or college can come back to tell students how they achieved success.	Arrange a class picnic at a local park with students' families.
Local community members, such as police officers, sanitation workers, or artists can answer questions about their important jobs and the tools they use.	Tour a local fire station, post office, police station, or library.
A dentist, doctor, nurse, PE teacher, or nutritionist can answer questions about dental hygiene, eating right, exercising, and staying healthy.	Plan a "get fit" day in the schoolyard or at a local park with fitness activities and healthy snacks.
A person living with a disability can discuss overcoming challenges.	Visit the local library where students can sign up for a library card and select books. A librarian can point out available resources.
Local leaders can talk about their work in the community and address students' questions or concerns.	Plan a visit to a local historical landmark or attend a local team's sporting event.
A scientist, detective, or anyone whose work involves looking closely can share discoveries that came from close examination.	Explore the schoolyard, a nearby park, or other area with a focus on learning through close observation.
A farmer or gardener can share how they grow plants for food.	Walk to a local grocery store, farmer's market, or community garden.
A zoologist or biologist can discuss animal habitats and answer questions about what animals need to live.	Take a nature walk to a nearby stream, pond, or city park to observe local animal habitats.

TEACHER → ↳ TO TEACHER
From the Classroom

"At back-to-school night, I survey children's families to ask if they have a job or hobby related to the topics we're going to study. My students are so motivated to learn when family members visit!"

Assessing Students Throughout the Year

Follow this suggested timeline to plan instruction and administer assessments throughout the course of the school year.

BEGINNING OF YEAR				MIDYEAR	
Module 1	Module 2	Module 3	Module 4	Module 5	Module 6

Module 1

	WEEK 1					WEEK 2	
	Lesson 1	Lesson 2	Lesson 3	Lesson 4	Lesson 5	Lesson 6	Lesson 7
Daily Formative Assessment	● ●	● ●	● ● ●	● ● ●	● ● ●	● ● ●	● ● ●
Guided Reading Benchmark Assessment Kit							
Intervention Assessments							
Selection Quizzes					●		●
Weekly Assessments					●		
Module Assessment							

Daily Formative Assessment

Use embedded opportunities for daily formative assessment along with Selection Quizzes. Then support or extend learning during small-group instruction.

- Vocabulary
- Reading Workshop
- Foundational Skills
- Writing Workshop

Intervention Assessments

- Use screener assessments at the beginning of the year.
- Follow up with diagnostic assessments for select students.
- Use progress-monitoring assessments every two weeks as needed.

Guided Reading Benchmark Assessment Kit

Use Benchmark Leveled Readers and oral reading records on an ongoing basis to assess students' reading skills.

		END OF YEAR			
Module 7	Module 8	Module 9	Module 10	Module 11	Module 12

WEEK 3							
Lesson **8**	Lesson **9**	Lesson **10**	Lesson **11**	Lesson **12**	Lesson **13**	Lesson **14**	Lesson **15**
• • • •	• • •	• • •	• • • •	• • •	• • • •	• • •	• • •

ASSESS LEARNING

Online

Weekly Assessments

Assess understanding of reading comprehension, vocabulary strategies, generative vocabulary, and grammar each week.

 36 Weekly Assessments per year

Module Assessments

Assess understanding of reading comprehension, vocabulary strategies, generative vocabulary, and writing and grammar.

 12 Module Assessments per year

Screening, Diagnostic, and Progress-Monitoring Assessments

Use these assessments to identify areas for intervention, plan flexible groups for teaching, and monitor progress throughout the year.

Grades 3–5 Intervention Assessments

ASSESSMENT TYPE	FREQUENCY	ASSESSED
Screening	• Beginning of year	• Oral Reading Fluency
Diagnostic	• Follow-up, as needed	• Letter-Sound Identification • Word Identification
Progress Monitoring	• Every two weeks, as needed	• Oral Reading Fluency

Screening Assessments

Use these assessments early in the school year to:

• obtain preliminary information about students' performance.

• screen all students for intervention.

• determine flexible groups for foundational skills instruction.

Oral Reading Fluency

Use the **Oral Reading Fluency** assessment to individually assess a student's oral reading skills. These tests focus on fluency, accuracy, and rate as well as provide important information about the student's decoding strategies by using specific grade-level targeted vocabulary.

Based on the results and other observations, determine whether students would benefit from intervention instruction or require additional diagnostic testing.

Diagnostic Assessments

Administer the diagnostic assessments as needed to:

- follow up with students who score below expectation on the screening assessments.

- obtain detailed information to inform skills-based flexible groups and targeted instruction.

Letter-Sound Correspondence

The **Letter-Sound Correspondence** assessment determines a student's ability to associate letters with sounds. Administer it by pointing to each letter and prompting the student to make the primary sound associated with the letter.

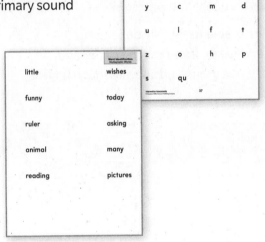

Word Identification

Use the **Word Identification** assessment to individually assess a student's ability to read high-frequency and multisyllabic words.

Progress-Monitoring Assessments

Administer these three- to five-minute oral assessments to individuals approximately every two weeks to:

- measure growth in pre-reading skills.

- identify challenging areas for reteaching, review, and extra practice.

- provide checks on students' beginning reading skills.

- monitor progress of students who are receiving intervention.

- help determine when students are ready to exit intervention.

 *Access the Intervention Assessments and more information online.*

Formative Assessments

Use formative assessments to determine students' mastery of skills and to plan for review, reteaching, or differentiation.

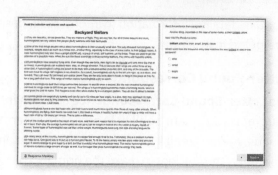

¡Arriba la Lectura! cuenta con todo esto y más. En la sección ¡Viva el español! verá lo que distingue a este programa.

Weekly and Module Assessments

The **Weekly and Module Assessments** measure students' understanding of major comprehension, vocabulary, and writing/grammar skills at the end of each week and module.

Each assessment has two sections:

- The **Reading** section assesses comprehension and vocabulary skills.

- The **Writing** section assesses grammar and writing skills.

Students may take the online assessments flexibly depending on your access to computers or devices. If you use the paper-and-pencil assessment, administer it as a group and allow as much time as students need to complete it.

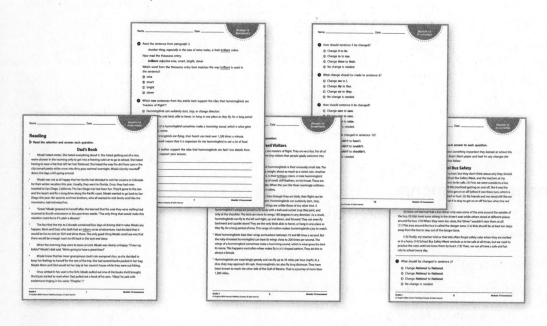

Online 😊**Ed** *Access guidelines and answer keys for the Weekly and Module Assessments online.*

Data Reports

When students take the Weekly and Module Assessments online, you can access **data reports** to analyze gaps and gains, form groups for differentiated instruction, and locate resources to target students' needs.

- **Assessment Report:** View class scores for each assessment and analyze student proficiency data.

- **Standards Report:** Follow students' progress in standards proficiency and access resources that support learning those skills.

Use data from the reports to:

- determine if students have met learning objectives for the week or module.

- look for patterns in students' errors to choose concepts and skills for reteaching or additional practice.

- decide if students are ready to advance to the next week or module of instruction.

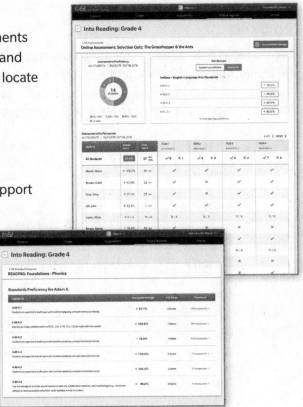

Formative Assessments

Targeted Skills

The lessons in Grades 3–5 include embedded opportunities for formative assessment during Targeted Skills Practice, as well as Selection Quizzes.

WEEK 1	WEEK 2	WEEK 3	TARGETED SKILLS PRACTICE
	Lesson 6	Lesson 11	Vocabulary
Lesson 1	Lesson 6	Lesson 11	Reading Skills and Strategies
Lesson 1	Lesson 6	Lesson 11	Foundational Skills
	Lesson 6	Lesson 11	Writing and Grammar
Lesson 2	Lesson 7	Lesson 12	Vocabulary
Lesson 2	Lesson 7	Lesson 12	Reading Skills and Strategies
Lesson 2		Lesson 12	Writing and Grammar
Lesson 3	Lesson 8	Lesson 13	Vocabulary
Lesson 3	Lesson 8	Lesson 13	Reading Skills and Strategies
Lesson 3	Lesson 8	Lesson 13	Foundational Skills
	Lesson 8	Lesson 13	Writing and Grammar
Lesson 4	Lesson 9	Lesson 14	Vocabulary
Lesson 4	Lesson 9	Lesson 14	Reading Skills and Strategies
	Lesson 9	Lesson 14	Writing and Grammar
Lesson 5	Lesson 10		Vocabulary
Lesson 5	Lesson 10	Lesson 15	Reading Skills and Strategies
	Lesson 10	Lesson 15	Writing and Grammar

Use each lesson's Independent Practice and Engage and Respond tasks to determine whether students are meeting the learning objectives. Depending on your observations, provide either support or extensions during Small-Group Instruction.

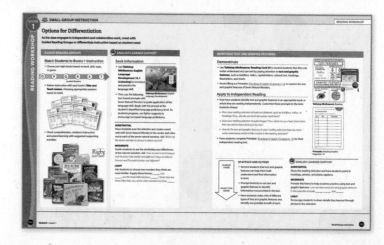

Benchmark Assessment Kit

Use the intermediate **Benchmark Assessment Kit** to determine students' guided reading levels and make instructional decisions.

The kit includes a paired fiction and nonfiction **Benchmark Leveled Reader** for guided reading levels J–W. Including this range of levels allows you to assess accelerated learners in your class beyond the grade-level expectation.

Follow the Teacher Directions in the corresponding **Benchmark Evaluation Guide** for guidance with:

- providing an overview of the selection.
- assessing oral reading by having the student read aloud while you mark errors.
- prompting the student to retell the selection.
- administering comprehension questions.
- using results to determine the student's guided reading level.

Conferring with Writers

As students write independently, circulate to ask questions, provide targeted feedback, and take notes to inform your teaching.

Encourage Writing Independence

Use these suggestions to ensure that students are engaged in writing, freeing you to have meaningful conversations.

- Talk about the expectations for independent writing with the class and revisit them if there is a breakdown during a session.

- Provide writing materials that are accessible, motivating, and developmentally appropriate.

- Anticipate issues that may draw your attention from conferring or distract students from their writing. For example, have a system in place for when students need to consult print or online reference sources.

- Teach students a set of **SILENT SIGNALS** (p. 53) to express their needs while you are conferring without interrupting a conference in progress.

- Encourage students to solve problems on their own or with peers using **ASK THREE, THEN ME** (p. 55).

- Give students strategies for common writing blockers, such as generating ideas or spelling words.

Conference Basics

During independent writing time, circulate and confer with a few students every day as time allows. A focused four- or five-minute conference gives you enough time to listen, deliver personalized instruction, and show students that you are paying attention.

Gather a set of portable materials to take as you meet with students. These may include a clipboard or notebook to document conferences, sticky notes, sharpened pencils, highlighters, and a stapler.

Let students know that you will be walking around the classroom while they write, and you may stop to talk to them about their writing.

When you approach students to confer:

- **Listen.** Look for what students are doing well, ask them about their writing, and listen to their response.

- **Affirm.** Based on what you hear, tell students something about the writing that is working well to reinforce their strengths.

- **Teach.** Focus on providing a general principle rather than a specific correction. Draw upon the focal text, writing model, or other familiar text to provide clear examples of the principle.

- **Apply.** Suggest that students try it themselves.

Document your conversations with students. Choose a system that works for you and matches your teaching style. You may decide to take notes in a notebook with a section for each student, on a clipboard, or on sticky notes to place in a notebook or directly in the student's writing folder. In your notes, include what is working well in the student's writing and an appropriate focus for the student to work on based on your conversation or your observations.

See page 91 for more ideas on observation notes.

Choosing Students for Conferences

You will likely have writers at all different stages of the writing process at any one time. So how do you decide which students to confer with? Here are some ideas:

- List a few students to target for conferences. Base your list on students' writing and your observations during small-group time. Also note students you haven't conferred with for a while or students who need a follow-up conference.

- Allow for some flexibility as you circulate to confer with students who signal for help. Scan work areas to ensure students are engaged.

- Target groups or individuals who need support to focus better. You may offer feedback to the class or a smaller group for the benefit of all within earshot.

- Use students' questions during independent writing to inform your teaching. When you notice there are a few students with similar needs, consider pulling them together for a small-group conference.

Language for Conferring

It can be challenging to think of meaningful feedback on the spot. You may find it helpful to compile a sheet of sample prompts, positive statements, questions, and teaching focuses based on your class's writing goals.

The Writing Workshop Revising lessons offer discussion ideas based on the module writing type and the daily lesson focus, but you can reference other lessons to support students who are working on a different step in the writing process.

Expectations for Conferring

At the beginning of the year, conferences may mostly reinforce the expectations for independent writing time or model how to access and share materials appropriately.

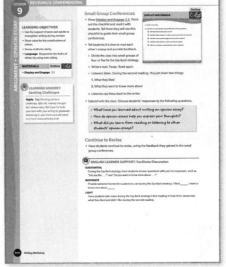

Writing Workshop Teacher's Guide

Some students may want to start by sketching their ideas. When you circulate, focus on how their sketches can transfer to written words:

- Reinforce the idea that pictures convey meaning and tell stories or organize information.

- Ask students to tell you about their sketches.

- Point out details you notice in students' sketches and encourage them to add details.

- Remind students to stay focused. Tell them that writers do their best and keep on writing.

Professional Learning

BEST PRACTICES

66 *If a teacher can listen to a writer talk about her writing, and then can skim what the child has done so far and intervene in ways that lift the level not only of this piece of writing but of that child's work on future pieces, that teacher's conferences are a Very Big Deal.* 99

— Calkins, Hartman & White (2005)

Assessing Writing and Projects

Use clear evaluation criteria to assess students' writing and project work and to provide actionable feedback.

Writing Rubrics

Use rubrics in the Resources section of the **Writing Workshop Teacher's Guide** or online to assess students' published opinion, narrative, informational text, and research writing in these areas:

- Organization and Presentation
- Development of Ideas
- Use of Language and Conventions

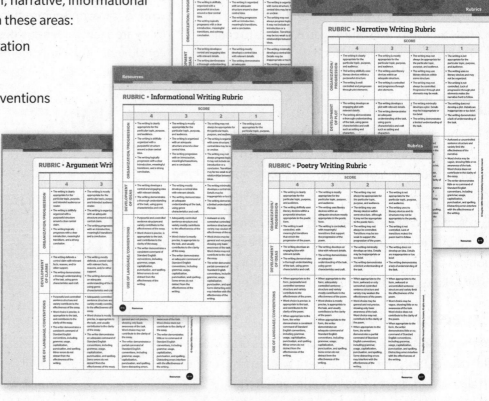

Inquiry and Research Project Rubric

Access the rubric in the Resources section of the **Writing Workshop Teacher's Guide** or online to assess students' project work from each module in four key areas:

- Collaboration
- Research and Text Evidence
- Content
- Presentation

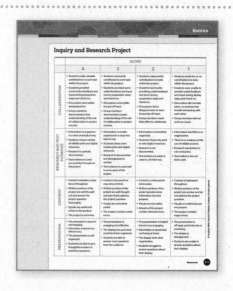

How to Use the Rubrics

Use specific criteria to monitor students' growth in writing types and project work throughout the year. Take notes to clarify scores and refer to during conferences.

1. Print the rubric from *Ed: Your Friend in Learning*, or copy the rubric from the **Writing Workshop Teacher's Guide.** Use a copy to score each student's work.

2. Review criteria for each area one at a time as you consider students' work.

3. Record a score for each criterion. Read the descriptors for each score, and consider which score best matches the student's performance.

4. Average scores for all of the criteria to determine an overall score of one to four.

Informational Writing Rubric

Rubric

		SCORE		
	4	**3**	**2**	**1**
ORGANIZATION/ PROGRESSION	• The writing is clearly appropriate for the particular topic, purpose, and audience. • The writing is skillfully organized with a purposeful structure around a clear central idea. • The writing logically progresses with a clear introduction, meaningful transitions, and a strong conclusion.	• The writing is mostly appropriate for the particular topic, purpose, and audience. • The writing is organized with an adequate structure around a clear central idea. • The writing progresses with an introduction, meaningful transitions, and a conclusion.	• The writing may not always be appropriate for the particular topic, purpose, and audience. • The writing is organized with some structure. The central idea may be weak or unclear. • The writing may not always progress logically. It may not include an introduction or a conclusion. Transitions may be too weak to show relationships between ideas.	• The writing is not appropriate for the particular topic, purpose, and audience. • The writing may not be organized. The central idea is missing or unclear. • The writing may not always progress. It may not include an introduction or a conclusion. Lack of transitions make the writing hard to follow.
DEVELOPMENT OF IDEAS	• The writing develops a central and engaging idea with relevant details. • The writing demonstrates a thorough understanding of the task, using genre characteristics and craft.	• The writing mostly develops a central idea with relevant details. • The writing demonstrates an adequate understanding of the task, using genre characteristics and craft.	• The writing minimally develops a central idea. Details may be inappropriate or too brief. • The writing demonstrates a limited understanding of the task.	• The writing does not develop a central idea. Details are inappropriate or too brief. • The writing demonstrates a lack of understanding of the task.
USE OF LANGUAGE/CONVENTIONS	• Purposeful and controlled sentence structure and variety contribute to the effectiveness of the essay. • Word choice is precise, is appropriate to the task, and contributes to the clarity of the essay. • The writer demonstrates a consistent command of Standard English conventions, including grammar, usage, capitalization, punctuation, and spelling. Minor errors do not detract from the effectiveness of the writing.	• Adequately controlled sentence structure and variety mostly contribute to the effectiveness of the essay. • Word choice is mostly precise, is appropriate to the task, and usually contributes to the clarity of the essay. • The writer demonstrates an adequate command of Standard English conventions, including grammar, usage, capitalization, punctuation, and spelling. Some errors do not detract from the effectiveness of the writing.	• Awkward or only somewhat controlled sentence structure and variety may weaken the effectiveness of the essay. • Word choice may be general and not precise, showing only basic awareness of the task. Word choice may not contribute to the clarity of the essay. • The writer demonstrates a partial command of Standard English conventions, including grammar, usage, capitalization, punctuation, and spelling. Some distracting errors may interfere with the effectiveness of the writing.	• Awkward or uncontrolled sentence structure and variety limit the effectiveness of the essay. • Word choice may be vague, showing little or no awareness of the task. Word choice does not contribute to the clarity of the essay. • The writer demonstrates little or no command of Standard English conventions, including grammar, usage, capitalization, punctuation, and spelling. Distracting errors interfere with the effectiveness of the writing.

Best Practices: Rubrics

- **Use anchor papers.** Identify work samples that exemplify particular scores for different rubric criteria, and reference these "anchor papers" if scoring questions arise.

- **Monitor growth.** Use rubric scores to track students' progress, and monitor their understanding of new skills and development of longer-term goals.

- **Be transparent.** Let students know the rubric criteria, and point out specific examples of what you will be looking for when you review their work.

- **Inform families.** Share students' work with families to highlight areas of growth. Give concrete examples of how families can provide support.

Documenting Students' Growth

Use informal assessment tools to gather data and gain a more complete picture of students' growth and instructional needs.

Portfolios

At the beginning of the year, set up portfolios for all of the students in your class. Some teachers compile portfolio contents in a binder for each student and designate a shelf in the classroom to store them. Other teachers use a hanging file folder for each student and house the portfolios in a storage crate.

Formal and Informal Assessments

Consider these suggestions for assessments to include in students' portfolios:

- Screening, Diagnostic, and Progress Monitoring Assessments (see pp. 80–81)

- Weekly Assessments and Module Assessments (see pp. 82–84)

- Writing Conferences (see pp. 86–87)

- Writing and Project Rubrics (see pp. 88–89)

- Observation Notes (see p. 91)

Work Samples

Collaborate with students to select work samples from their portfolios that showcase their best work and document growth over the year. These samples may include:

- *my*Book work, such as response writing, vocabulary networks, or knowledge maps.

- completed Reading or Language Graphic Organizers.

- keyboarding samples from the beginning, middle, and end of the year.

- writing samples of different writing forms over the course of the year.

- photos of students' inquiry and research projects or other collaborative work.

Reading Surveys

Survey students and their families at the beginning and middle of the year to gather information about their reading interests, attitudes, and preferences.

Use the information from surveys to inform instructional planning, support students with self-selected reading, and recommend books or literacy routines to families. Have students complete a Reading Log for their independent reading. Use it to monitor students' reading frequency and what they record about their reading.

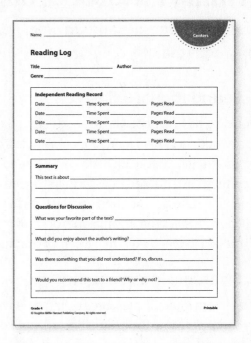

Observation Notes

Observe students closely, and take notes during individual conferences, guided reading groups, small-group instruction, and independent reading and writing.

Set up a system for recording and organizing observation notes that works for you. One option is keeping a clipboard handy to take notes throughout the day. Another option is using a file folder with sticky notes to record observations for each student. Once you have recorded observations, transfer your notes to students' individual portfolios.

You may consider observing and noting:

- reading behaviors students show during guided reading, such as rereading or self-correcting.

- writing strategies students use independently, such as adding details, applying grammar skills, or correcting spelling errors.

- examples of students displaying social-emotional skills, such as responsible decision making, social awareness, self-awareness, and self-management, or using relationship skills.

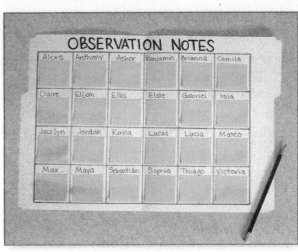

Forming Flexible Groups

Make the most of small-group time by using data to thoughtfully form groups that will optimize student growth.

¡Arriba la Lectura! cuenta con todo esto y más. En la sección ¡Viva el español! verá lo que distingue a este programa.

Foundational Skills

Students come to school with a range of foundational skills knowledge. Using assessment data to plan foundational skills lessons will allow you to provide more targeted attention based on need and will keep advanced learners from tiring of lessons they have mastered. Assess all students at the beginning of the year using Intervention Assessments, and use the data to plan lessons. Use whole-class instruction for skills that the majority of students have not mastered. Form flexible small groups to teach skills that a cohort of students need to learn or review.

Strategic Intervention

Use data from multiple measures to implement daily targeted Tier 2 and Tier 3 interventions during designated times. Depending on resources in your school and students' individual needs, strategic intervention may be a combination of pull-out, push-in, small-group, or one-to-one time.

For more information on assessment and resources for intervention, see pages 80–81 and 106–107.

Small-Group Instruction

Use data to form flexible small groups and locate resources for differentiation.

SMALL GROUP	ASSESSMENT DATA	INSTRUCTIONAL RESOURCES
Guided Reading	• Guided Reading Benchmark Assessment Kit • Oral Reading Records • Adaptive Growth Measure and Student Growth Report • Leveled Reader Quizzes	• Rigby Leveled Readers • Take and Teach Lessons • Tabletop Minilessons: Reading
English Language Support	• State English Language Development Assessments	• Tabletop Minilessons: English Language Development • English Language Support lessons • Language Graphic Organizers
Skills and Strategies	• Daily Formative Assessments • Weekly Assessments	• Tabletop Minilessons: Reading • Reinforce Skills and Strategies lessons • Reading Graphic Organizers
Foundational Skills	• Informal Assessments	• Foundational Skills lessons • Foundational Skills and Word Study Studio

Small-Group Weekly Schedule

Plan a weekly schedule for small-group instruction based on the individual needs of students in your classroom. Every school and class is different, so no two small-group schedules will be alike. Use the sample below as a model for creating your own.

SMALL GROUPS WEEK 15	MONDAY	TUESDAY	WEDNESDAY	THURSDAY	FRIDAY
Guided Reading 15 minutes	Level O	Level P	Level Q	Level R	Level S
English Language Development 15 minutes	Seek Information	Seek Information	Seek Information	Seek Information	Seek Information
Reinforce Skills and Strategies 15 minutes	Text and Graphic Features	Synthesize	Central Idea	Text Structure	Text and Graphic Features

Online Ed Customized Groups

Create and track small groups online based on assessment and observational data.

- *Ed: Your Friend in Learning* will automatically group students based on *Into Reading* assessment results.

- Customize your groups using drag and drop functionality.

- Click each student's name to view more information.

Online Ed Resources for Small-Group Instruction

Access recommended resources online for each group, or search for your own based on individual needs. Then assign resources to groups to create a customized small-group plan.

- **View** recommended resources for each group.

- **Search** for additional resources as needed.

- **Assign** resources to groups or individuals.

Supporting English Learners

Building your own understanding of students' first languages and the stages of second language acquisition can help you determine appropriate levels of scaffolding and targeted language support.

¡Arriba la Lectura! cuenta con todo esto y más. En la sección ¡Viva el español! verá lo que distingue a este programa.

Stages of Second Language Acquisition

Students progress through five stages as they acquire English language skills.

STAGE	CHARACTERISTICS OF LEARNERS
❶ **Preproduction**	• silence or speaking exclusively in first language • ability to mimic but not produce original thoughts in new language • characterized by observing and listening • learn through gestures, images, or other visual aids
❷ **Early Production**	• use of simple sentences and phrases • repetition of learned phrases or "headlines" • use of verbs in present tense • ability to answer simple questions
❸ **Speech Emergence**	• ability to use English to communicate and learn • communication in simple sentences with frequent errors • dependence on context clues and familiar subject matter for comprehension
❹ **Intermediate Fluency**	• fluent communication in academic and social settings • few grammatical errors but some vocabulary gaps • ability to understand some figurative language, make predictions and comparisons, and formulate explanations
❺ **Advanced Fluency**	• effective communication about a variety of subjects • vocabulary comparable to that of a native speaker • may still use idioms incorrectly or speak with an accent

Professional Learning

RESEARCH FOUNDATIONS

❝ *Children's language skills in kindergarten predict their performance in other areas, including math and reading, throughout school. Not only does a child's use of vocabulary and grammar predict future proficiency with the spoken and written word, but it also affects performance in other subject areas.* ❞

—Echart (2018)

English Learner Support

Into Reading lessons have embedded **English Learner Support** for multiple language proficiency levels across instructional contexts. Look for the recurring feature along the bottom section of your Teacher's Guide lessons.

Preview the strategies before teaching a lesson and select the level of support and strategy that best targets the needs of the English learners in your class.

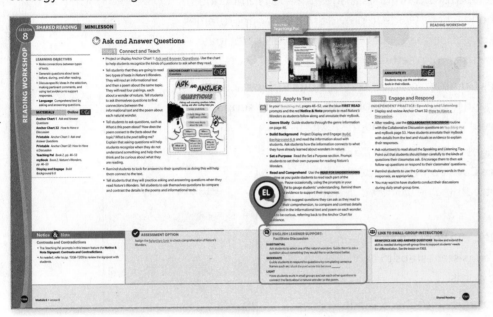

Small-Group Support

Depending on the number of English learners in your class and the level of support that they require, form small groups for English language support.

If most students in your class are English learners, and the level of support they need varies, you may decide to form multiple small groups. If you have six or fewer English learners, you may decide to form one group but provide different levels of support within it.

During daily small-group English Learner Support:

- use the **Tabletop Minilessons: English Language Development** to introduce, review, and practice a particular language function.

- use the text-based prompts in the Teacher's Guide to practice the language function in the context of the daily reading.

See page 33 for more information about materials for English language support.

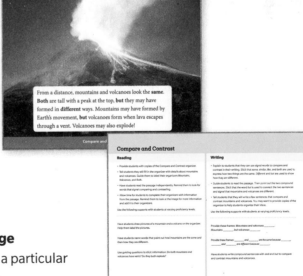

Supporting English Learners

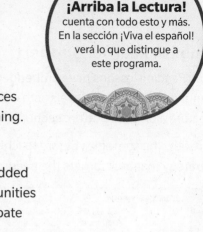

¡Arriba la Lectura! cuenta con todo esto y más. En la sección ¡Viva el español! verá lo que distingue a este programa.

Effective Instruction to Build Language

Into Reading for Grades 3 to 5 embeds evidence-based strategies and practices that contribute to all students' learning while also accelerating English learning.

These strategies and practices include:

- **Engage students.** Use the ENGAGEMENT routines (pages 148–151) embedded throughout the lessons in the Teacher's Guide to provide frequent opportunities for English learners at all stages of language acquisition to actively participate and respond verbally in a low-risk group setting.

- **Build knowledge.** Teacher's Guide lessons and **Get Curious Videos** activate and build students' background knowledge about module topics to support their understanding of concepts, vocabulary, and the texts.

- **Make learning visual.** Images on **Vocabulary Cards Anchor Charts,** and **Picture Cards** provide students with a visual reference to support learning new concepts, words, and skills.

- **Teach vocabulary explicitly.** The VOCABULARY routine and **Vocabulary Cards** include consistent steps to explicitly teach module topic and academic words.

- **Bolster word-learning strategies.** Teacher's Guide lessons focus on strategies for determining word meaning and exploring word relationships.

- **Read texts multiple times.** Teacher's Guide lessons and routines engage students in multiple readings of texts in whole class and in smaller group settings.

- **Provide sentence frames.** Teacher's Guide lessons include sentence frames to support students as they structure their verbal and written responses.

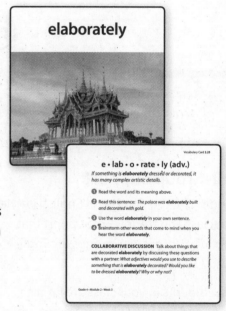

Vocabulary Cards

Best Practices: English Learners

Keep these best practices in mind as you plan how to best meet the needs of the English learners in your class:

- Include English learners in all lessons and class activities. Ensure that students who receive "pull-out" services don't miss critical content.

- Demonstrate respect for and interest in students' first languages—for example, by asking them to share the equivalent of an English word.

- Work to build a non-intimidating environment in which students feel free to take risks.

- Use pictures, visual aids, and gestures paired with words whenever possible, especially when giving directions and when teaching lessons.

- Demonstrate or act out procedures, vocabulary, and stories as a class to help English learners access information. For example, have students practice prepositions for location with an object, such as an eraser at their desks. Tell students to put the eraser *on* the desk, *in* the desk, *under* the desk, *above* the desk, and *beside* the desk.

- Make the most of teachable moments by pointing out differences in pronunciation, meaning, and spelling of words when students encounter them. For example, minimal pairs (e.g., *check, chick*), multiple-meaning words (e.g., *sink*), and homophones (e.g., *pear, pair*).

- Take students' efforts to communicate seriously and assure them that making mistakes is to be expected and is part of the learning process.

● Professional Learning

RESEARCH FOUNDATIONS

❝ *Making the core curriculum comprehensible is central to preventing new English learners from becoming long-term English learners.* ❞

— Echevarria, Frey & Fisher (2015)

Supporting English Learners

Addressing Language Differences

Students who speak a language other than English bring with them knowledge of language to use as building blocks for learning English. Understanding similarities and differences between a student's first language and English can help guide and tailor your instruction to meet students' individual needs.

Helpful Similarities

Students will naturally compare and contrast English with their first language and use that knowledge to develop English language skills. Students' first languages can provide useful tools to help them learn English and act as a familiar frame of reference.

Learning cognates is one way to draw on a shared element to help strengthen students' vocabulary. Cognates are words that are written and pronounced similarly between languages, e.g., *attention* in English and *atención* in Spanish. Shared letter-sound correspondences (e.g., the letter *d* stands for the sound /d/ in both Spanish and English) are another example of a shared element that can help students as they learn to read and write in English. As you consider how to best support English learners in your class, keep in mind that cognates are only useful if students already have an understanding of the word in their first language.

Contrasting Differences

When elements of a student's first language conflict with elements of English, it can cause confusion that impedes English learning. For example, false cognates can lead to attributing incorrect meaning to words. False cognates are words that are spelled or pronounced very similarly across languages but mean very different things, such as *exit* in English and *éxito*, which means *success* in Spanish. These words appear to be very similar but have two very different meanings!

Non-Correlated Elements

When language learners encounter a feature of English that is not present in their first language, or vice-versa, it neither helps nor harms their acquisition of English. For example, articles do not exist as parts of speech in Vietnamese, so students whose first language is Vietnamese will have no frame of reference for using the word *the*. Some sounds in English may not exist in students' first language. In those cases, students may need additional practice with mouth positions and articulating sounds.

Building Cross-Linguistic Connections

Use *Into Reading* resources to build cross-linguistic connections between English and students' first languages.

The **Language Differences** resource can help you understand differences between students' first languages and English. The languages featured in the online resource are:

- Spanish
- Vietnamese
- Cantonese and Mandarin
- Filipino
- Hmong
- Korean

This resource gives specific examples comparing these languages to English. It can help you target specific areas that are challenging and identify areas in which students can leverage knowledge from their first languages.

Use the resource to become familiar with ways that each language aligns with or differs from English in the following areas:

- Alphabet (Writing System)
- Phonological Features (Consonant and Vowel Sounds)
- Grammatical Features (Parts of Speech, Verb Tenses, Sentence Structure and Syntax)

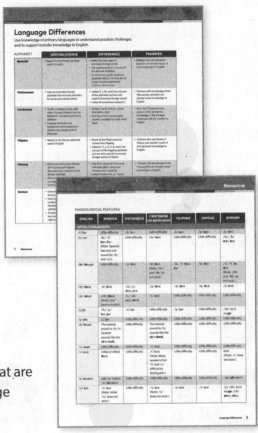

Dual Language and Biliteracy

¡Arriba la Lectura! cuenta con todo esto y más. En la sección ¡Viva el español! verá lo que distingue a este programa.

Purpose-Built Equity and Support

¡Arriba la Lectura! is a Spanish Reading and Language Arts program intentionally created to be used in conjunction with *Into Reading* in dual language and biliteracy settings. The program is designed around high-interest, knowledge-building module topics that follow a parallel structure to the modules in *Into Reading*. This provides teachers with complementary resources to reinforce students' content and language learning in English and Spanish. Skill and concept development align across the programs, except where linguistic differences call for appropriate instructional differences (such as for foundational skill development).

The daily Cross-Linguistic Bridge and Dual Language Settings features in the *¡Arriba la Lectura!* **Teacher Guide** support teachers in establishing connections between Spanish and English in every lesson. These resources provide tools to encourage bilingual learning and support students' cognitive development in both languages.

Dual Language Implementation Guide

Guia del maestro

Teacher's Guide

miLibra

myBook

Dual Language Implementation Guide

The **Dual Language Implementation Guide** was conceived by program author Dr. Elena Izquierdo, an expert in dual language and biliteracy. Its purpose is to help teach and implement dual language and biliteracy programs. It gives teachers opportunities to combine material from *¡Arriba la Lectura!* and *Into Reading* efficiently and easily with great flexibility, following the goals of their selected dual language model. The guide is divided into three parts, designed to provide easy access for teachers to consult on an ongoing basis, with an attractive bilingual design for ease of reading and navigation.

Part 1: Language Acquisition in Bilingual Environments

This section introduces basic concepts in biliteracy, such as the various models of bilingual education and their common principles, the development of cultural awareness, and translanguaging. It introduces a theoretical framework for teachers that provides the rationale for the relevance of dual language instruction and informs the overall instructional approach. This section also includes a bilingual glossary of professional terms and a bibliography of relevant research related to Spanish learning, bilingualism, dual language, and biliteracy.

Support for district leaders and teachers in maintaining and extending an inclusive, student-centered culture in which biliteracy can thrive.

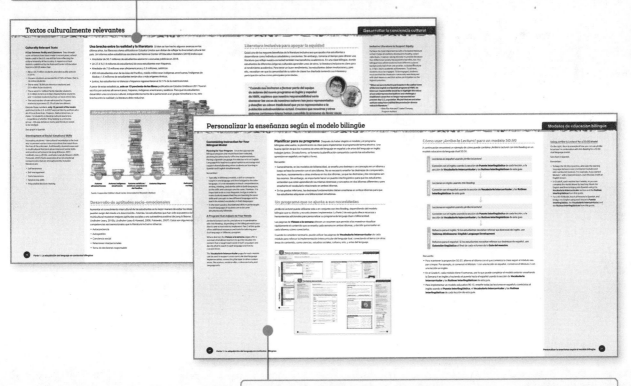

Practical suggestions for classroom management in dual language and other bilingual settings.

Part 2: Planning for the Grade

Part 2 provides grade-specific resources for efficient lesson planning.

Dual Language Across the Curriculum Cross-Curricular Vocabulary sections for each module include definitions, examples of usage, and suggested activities. Suggested activities are designed to expand vocabulary, to further develop module-specific content knowledge, and to support cross-curricular connections in both languages.

> Many dual language programs extend across the curriculum; the Dual Language Implementation Guide supports vocabulary bridging science, health, social studies, and the arts.

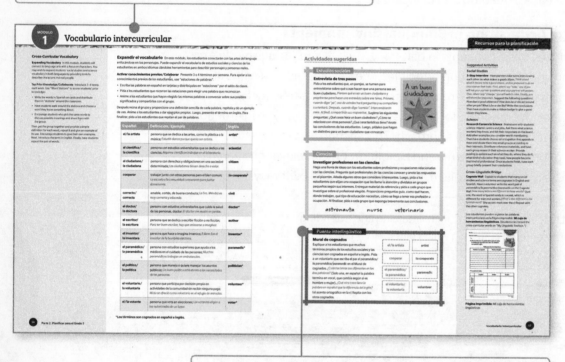

> The Cross-Linguistic Bridge section suggests ideas for cognate walls that support students in making connections between the two languages.

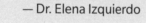

66 *Academic language is different from everyday language.* **99**

— Dr. Elena Izquierdo

Week at a Glance The At a Glance section provides an easy-to-read display of the content taught every week in both languages. This resource supports teachers in the intentional selection of instructional topics for each language and in the design of the connections between the English and Spanish instruction.

> Week at a Glance provides a dual scope and sequence from which teaching teams (Spanish and English) can decide what to teach in Spanish, what to teach in English, and how to bridge between the two. An overview of each week's Cross-Linguistic Bridges is included.

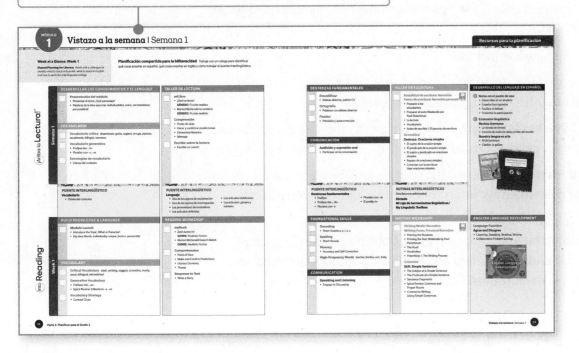

Additional Resources

The third part of the **Dual Language Implementation Guide** contains routines, rubrics, and planning templates to support the implementation of *¡Arriba la Lectura!* and *Into Reading* in dual language and biliteracy programs. This section also provides the resources to support the implementation of a dictation routine. The dictation routine provides structured and controlled practice in which students apply the language arts content that they have learned each week. The dictation routine also provides the opportunity for students to reflect on their language learning and compare and contrast the two languages to develop their metalinguistic awareness.

Implementing a Multi-tiered System of Supports

A strong, multi-tiered system of supports ensures all students receive the support they need to be successful learners.

What Is a Multi-tiered System of Supports?

Multi-tiered System of Supports (MTSS) is a process of systematically documenting student performance and providing instruction and interventions matched to student need, monitoring progress frequently, and applying data to educational decisions.

Successful MTSS frameworks include:

- **Assessment:** Screening, diagnostic, and progress-monitoring assessments track students' progress against grade-level expectations.

- **Data-Driven Decision Making:** Intervention based on assessment data and resources with selected supports to meet the individual needs of each student.

- **Differentiated Instruction:** Core instruction review, targeted group intervention, or more intensive intervention, depending on students' demonstrated level of need.

- **Behavioral Supports:** Application of instruction and support to prevent inappropriate behavior by teaching and reinforcing appropriate behaviors, based on students' demonstrated level of need.

Using Data to Drive Decision Making

The first step is assessment. Different types of assessment can help educators and administrators identify areas in which students need additional support.

- **Screening:** Students should be screened to assess their academic performance against grade-level standards.

- **Diagnostic:** Students whose initial assessment scores show a particular area of concern should receive diagnostic assessments to determine where intervention is needed.

- **Progress Monitoring:** Ongoing progress monitoring should be used to measure the effectiveness of instruction or interventions.

For more information on intervention assessments, see pages 106–107.

● *Professional Learning*

RESEARCH FOUNDATIONS

❝ *Tier-2 interventions produce meaningful effects on student reading achievement in schools experiencing persistently low reading achievement and across very different school districts.* ❞

— Coyne et al. (2018)

Determining the Appropriate Level of Intervention

Response to Intervention (RtI) is a critical part of the larger MTSS framework. RtI is a multi-level system for maximizing student achievement by using assessment data to help determine the appropriate level of intervention for each student.

RtI organizes intervention into tiers of increasingly intense interventions for those students who are not making adequate progress with core instruction or after changes in instruction. The level of intervention is intensified, as needed, by:

- increasing instructional time.
- decreasing group sizes.
- matching materials to students' skill levels.
- providing corrective feedback.

Three Tiers of Intervention Support

TIER III

Intensive Intervention

- Individualized instruction and pacing
- Assessment-based, high intensity, longer duration intervention in a small-group, one-to-one, push-in, or pull-out setting

TIER II

Strategic Intervention

- Supplemental curricula for some students who are not successful with Tier I instruction
- Explicit, rapid-response, short-term instruction in a small-group setting

TIER I

Core Instruction

- Universal preventative, proactive interventions for all students
- Small-group instruction for key grade-level skills

Providing Differentiated Support and Intervention

Choose flexible resources based on students' assessed needs to provide the appropriate level of support.

Guided Reading Groups

Choose books that match students' instructional levels and target specific reading behaviors to reinforce whole-group skills.

- Use the **Guided Reading Benchmark Assessment** to determine students' instructional level for guided reading groups.

- Reinforce or intervene by choosing just-right books from a library of 570 **Leveled Readers** from across the spectrum of guided reading levels.

- Select flexible teaching sessions from the **Take and Teach Lessons** to deliver scaffolded instruction while meeting with guided reading groups.

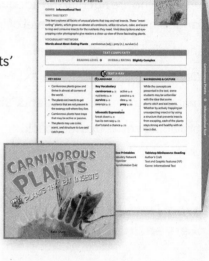

Reading Skill and Strategy Support

Teach a skill or strategy that students have not yet mastered or connect to the day's whole-group skill with scaffolded support to reinforce learning.

- Reinforce the skill from whole-group Reading and Vocabulary using the **Scaffold and Extend** options in your Teacher's Guide.

- Intervene based on data and reteach grade-level skills or strategies using accessible texts and the Almost There prompts on **Tabletop Minilessons: Reading.**

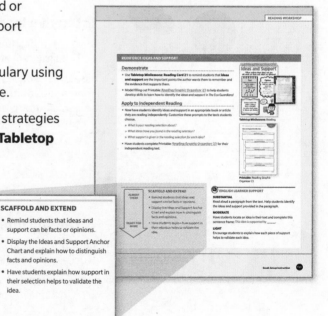

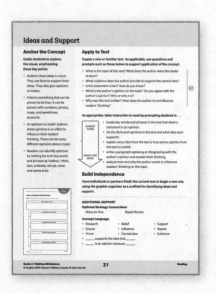

Foundational Skills Support

Teach prerequisite foundational skills or reinforce daily foundational skills lessons during small-group or one-to-one time.

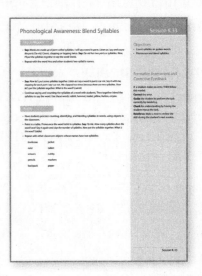

- Use the **Intervention Assessments** to determine which prerequisite Foundational Skills students need to learn or review.

- Intervene using the appropriate lessons from the **Foundational Skills and Word Study Studio.**

Best Practices: Intervention Support

Follow these best practices to plan and provide differentiated support and intervention.

- **Screen and diagnose.** Screen students at the beginning of the year to identify any areas for which they may need additional support. Then follow up with diagnostic assessments for select students.

- **Assess.** Use frequent and multiple measures to guide instructional decisions and monitor progress throughout the year.

- **Individualize.** Provide individualized support and learning strategies based on the student's needs and most successful learning approaches.

- **Set goals.** Establish goals for students and track progress. Discuss goals with students and their families and celebrate achievements along the way.

- **Locate resources.** Use *Ed: Your Friend in Learning* to find resources recommended based on students' assessment data. Search for resources by skill or standard.

- **Provide feedback.** When possible, provide students with immediate corrective feedback.

- **Share information.** Connect with other teachers, administrators, and families to build a team of support for each student. Meet regularly to share assessment data and discuss progress.

Using Digital Features for Accessibility

Access digital features to assist you as you work with students who have impairments to vision, hearing, cognition, or mobility.

Content Accessibility

Web Content Accessibility Guidelines (WCAG) provide recommendations for making digital tools and technologies accessible for people with disabilities. *Ed: Your Friend in Learning* follows WCAG 2.0 AA recommendations to meet the needs of diverse learners.

ACCESSIBILITY FEATURE	IMPAIRMENT			
	VISUAL	HEARING	COGNITIVE	MOBILITY
closed captioning for videos		●	●	
transcripts for audio	●	●	●	
contrast and color compliance	●		●	
screen reader compatibility (keyboard operability) for platform and content	●		●	●
keyboard encoding for compatibility with many assistive technologies	●	●	●	●
responsive, reflowable design	●	●	●	●
pedagogically equivalent alternatives for components and resources	●	●	●	●

Inclusive Design and Compassionate Innovation

Additional built-in features create an engaging and instructionally effective experience for all students. These features include:

- read-along audio with synchronized text highlighting.
- tools for student highlighting and note-taking.
- point-of-use glossary entries.
- custom planning features.
- Spanish language.
- pedagogical text alternatives.
- curiosity-provoking and engaging text alternatives.
- grade- and level-appropriate text alternatives.

Text Alternatives

When texts include images as part of the learning experience, *Into Reading* and *¡Arriba la Lectura!* use text alternatives that strive to convey the same experience to all students, including those using assistive technologies, such as screen readers. These thoughtful, pedagogically sound, and engaging text alternatives provide equity in learning for all students.

Informational Texts

Informational texts include text alternatives for diagrams, maps, portraits, or other images. Here is a Grade 4 *my*Book example:

1 In the diagram for "Smell," the accompanying text does not convey the positional relationships, so the text alternative provides this information: *In this cross-section of a human head, an aroma is shown entering the nose. Deep inside the nose is the olfactory nerve. Deeper still is a nasal cavity.*

2 The text above the diagram for "Sight" includes the positional information shown in the diagram, so the text alternative is more general: *A diagram of an eyeball showing lens, retina, and optic nerve.*

3 The text in the "Taste" section doesn't describe the positions of the labels in the diagram, so the text alternative provides that information: *This diagram shows areas of the tongue where specific flavors are tasted. Sweet is picked up by the tip of the tongue, salty by the sides in front, sour by the sides in back, and bitter at the very back of the tongue.*

Literature

Text alternatives go beyond the basics to create equity in engagement as well. Story illustrations have text alternatives that share important details and strive to create the same engagement for students using screen readers as their peers enjoy.

Here is a Grade 1 eBook example:

Tall city apartment buildings crowd together. Below, a taxicab honks. Music plays from an open window, and an air conditioner hums. The people who live in the apartments are talking, eating, and watching television with their windows open. An ice cream shop is open for business.

Meeting the Needs of Special Populations

Build an understanding of the unique challenges some students face to help you make decisions about how best to support their learning.

Understand and Address Challenges

Many districts use a Multi-tiered System of Supports, which is designed to ensure timely, targeted interventions for students who struggle. The first requirement for all students, regardless of ability or disability, is an evidence-based, engaging core curriculum, with differentiation in pacing and grouping strategies for those who need more support.

While students with challenges may require different levels of intervention throughout the school day, ensure that *all* students have opportunities to:

• participate in whole-class discussions and projects.

• demonstrate standards-based learning via multiple assessment measures.

• strive for learning goals and receive instruction based on achievement data.

Challenge: Concept Knowledge and Oral Language

Some students have limited concept knowledge or oral language, which may be a result of weak word-reading skills. Students who struggle with reading read less and do not reap the knowledge and language growth that come from extensive reading.

INSTRUCTIONAL FOCUS	SUPPORT IN *INTO READING* AND *¡ARRIBA LA LECTURA!*
• Build background knowledge about concepts and content-area topics. • Directly teach academic vocabulary related to a topic or theme. • Encourage students to interact with words. • Provide scaffolds, such as sentence frames, to facilitate students' participation in class discussions. • Honor and validate students' home languages, and explicitly teach and model the language of school.	• **Get Curious Videos, Module Posters, Knowledge Maps,** and lessons support students to build knowledge networks. • A **VOCABULARY** routine, **Vocabulary Cards,** and Teacher's Guide lessons include steps to teach and practice using topic and academic words from texts. • Vocabulary and Writing Workshop lessons guide students to use new words in speaking and writing. • Lessons include sentence frames to support students in structuring oral and written responses. • Social communication and collaborative discussion lessons explicitly teach and guide practice of speaking and listening skills.

Challenge: Dyslexia and Word-reading Skills

Some students have dyslexia, a specific learning disability that involves difficulties in phonological processing. These difficulties make it hard for students to develop phonemic awareness, or the ability to identify and manipulate the smallest sounds of speech, which, in turn, makes decoding extremely difficult. A lack of fluent decoding generally leads to low levels of academic vocabulary and understanding of language structures due to insufficient exposure to academic texts.

Students who do not have a diagnosed disability may *also* have difficulties with phonological processing and word-level reading, the most common impediments to fluent word reading. *Into Reading* and *¡Arriba la Lectura!* include instruction and supports to address challenges students may have with these skills.

INSTRUCTIONAL FOCUS	SUPPORT IN *INTO READING* AND *¡ARRIBA LA LECTURA!*
• Provide daily, engaging instruction in phonemic awareness. • Systematically work with students on phoneme segmenting and blending. • Directly build automatic recognition of high-frequency words. • Practice new skills and review previously learned ones through daily reading of connected texts. • Include daily opportunities for small-group instruction and practice to differentiate instruction for the range of student needs in the class.	• Use targeted lessons from the **Foundational Skills and Word Study Studio** to develop automaticity in decoding and morphological knowledge and to provide extended practice in advanced phoneme manipulation and writing words with common but challenging spelling patterns. • Foundational Skills lessons follow an evidence-based scope and sequence including blending and segmenting phonemes. • Provide small-group instruction for Foundational Skills, as needed, and for Guided Reading as options for teaching and practicing various skills in small groups.

Meeting the Needs of Special Populations

Challenge: Visual, Hearing, Physical, or Cognitive Disabilities

INSTRUCTIONAL FOCUS	SUPPORT IN *INTO READING* AND *¡ARRIBA LA LECTURA!*
• Provide multiple options to help students understand, participate, respond, and express themselves.	• The instructional model includes whole-class lessons, small-group instruction, and options for building independence.
• Allow for variations in the pace of lessons and in the length of time spent on a given skill or concept.	• Daily lessons are organized so that teachers can adjust pacing and schedules as needed.
• Establish routines and set goals to support students in building executive function skills.	• Consistent routines and procedures across lessons help students know what to expect.
• Vary options for expressing understanding and ideas: verbal and nonverbal, visual and nonvisual.	• Resources allow students to set and monitor reading and writing goals.
• Limit the amount of sensory stimulation in the classroom.	• Engagement and classroom routines provide options for expression. For example, the **SILENT SIGNALS** routine allows students to respond and demonstrate understanding nonverbally.
• When available and appropriate, provide students with braille formats and supports using American Sign Language.	• Suggestions for setting up the classroom include minimizing artificial light and unnecessary visual stimulation.
• Provide features to make digital content, including videos and eBook texts, accessible to students with disabilities.	• HMH supports the mission of the NIMAC, which distributes NIMAS files for core student print materials to state and local education agencies to facilitate the creation of large print, braille, or other accessible formats.
	• The digital content on *Ed: Your Friend in Learning* includes WCAG 2.0 AA compliance features, such as closed captioning for videos, contrast and color compliance, responsive and reflowable design, and pedagogically equivalent text alternatives.

See pages 108–109 for more information about accessibility features available online.

Challenge: Engagement in Learning

Students who struggle with reading may cope by not engaging and may appear unmotivated—especially if they perceive there is no possibility for them to succeed. All students, without exception, need encouragement and validation to become successful, lifelong learners. *Into Reading* and *¡Arriba la Lectura!* include content and instruction that engage and nurture the whole child in learning.

INSTRUCTIONAL FOCUS	SUPPORT IN *INTO READING* AND *¡ARRIBA LA LECTURA!*
• Consider the whole child and social-emotional learning that is critical for each student's development. • Ensure that students participate in whole-class and small-group instruction. • Actively engage students through interactive reading and writing strategies. • Explore topics and provide texts that are suited to students' skill levels and interests. • Provide clear and specific feedback. • Guide students to set goals. • Promote choice to build autonomy, decision-making skills, and independence.	• Lessons make connections to social-emotional learning and include embedded support for fostering growth mindset beliefs. • Engagement routines, such as **ECHO READING** and **TURN AND TALK**, allow all students opportunities to participate and respond. • Shared reading, dialogic reading, and group projects involve students in actively responding to texts and working together to contribute to shared written texts. • Captivating content and high-quality, grade-appropriate texts seek to ignite a lifelong love of learning. • Correct and Redirect features in Foundational Skills lessons and support for conferring with students during Writing Workshop guide teachers to give immediate, targeted feedback. • Students set and monitor their own reading and writing goals. • Literacy Centers give students opportunities to make choices about activities, materials, partners, and seating.

Meeting the Needs of Accelerated Learners

Provide targeted support to students who are exceeding grade-level expectations to keep them engaged and thriving.

Who Are Accelerated Learners?

Accelerated learners are students whose skills are above grade-level. They may not have been identified as "gifted," but they are clearly ready for accelerated learning experiences, such as more challenging books to read, more writing opportunities, and leadership roles in group projects.

With heavy emphasis placed on reaching students who are trailing behind their peers, accelerated learners sometimes sit through day after day of lessons for skills they have already mastered. When accelerated learners are disengaged, they can become restless, act out, and even begin to dislike school, making it critical to provide them with learning opportunities matched to their abilities.

Ready for More

Daily options for differentiation in *Into Reading* and *¡Arriba la Lectura!* provide support for accelerated learners who are ready for more, including the following:

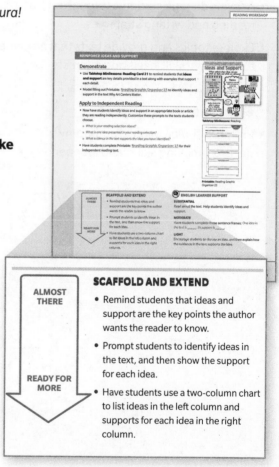

- Teaching support labeled **Ready for More** extends skill and strategy work during small-group lessons and provides daily opportunities for those students who need a challenge.

- **Rigby Leveled Readers** and **Leveled Reading Cards** with **Take and Teach Lessons** may be used to support Guided Reading groups.

- **Tabletop Minilessons: Reading** provide support as students apply comprehension skills to higher-level texts they are reading independently.

- **Inquiry and Research Projects** and **Reading Remake** activities in every module provide opportunities for enrichment.

SCAFFOLD AND EXTEND

ALMOST THERE

READY FOR MORE

- Remind students that ideas and support are the key points the author wants the reader to know.

- Prompt students to identify ideas in the text, and then show the support for each idea.

- Have students use a two-column chart to list ideas in the left column and supports for each idea in the right column.

Avoid Assumptions

Carefully consider ways to avoid making incorrect assumptions that could impact accelerated learners in your class.

- Advanced abilities may not cut across all content areas. For example, a student who reads above level may be a reluctant writer or need scaffolding in math.

- Having classroom library books that span the expected range for your grade-level is not enough. Provide a range of texts that mirror the range of reading abilities of the students in your class.

- Assigning additional work to accelerated learners, such as asking them to write more than classmates, will not effectively meet their needs. Instead, provide an alternate, more challenging version of the activity for enrichment.

- Unexpected or challenging behaviors may be a result of an accelerated learner lacking engaging work at the appropriate level.

- Differentiation doesn't have to happen in small groups. While small-group time might be the most obvious setting for supporting accelerated learners, increase engagement and minimalize behavioral challenges by looking for opportunities to differentiate for accelerated learners in whole-class settings as well.

Best Practices: Accelerated Learners

Remember these best practices when working with accelerated learners:

- Use flexible grouping and avoid forming fixed groups for extended periods of time. Students may be above level for particular skills but not for others, or be above level at one point in the year but not remain so.

- Provide opportunities for students to make their own decisions whenever possible. Think of ways for accelerated learners to take on leadership roles and assist classmates, when appropriate.

- Provide targeted feedback to accelerated learners based on their learning goals—just as you do with their peers.

●─ *Professional Learning*

RESEARCH FOUNDATIONS

66 *Teachers must observe and note the progress of students to know how to adjust instruction to keep the accelerated students engaged and motivated while providing additional support as needed.* 99

— Hougen (2012)

Building Knowledge Networks

Students build networks of knowledge that help them construct meaning.

What Is a Knowledge Network?

A **knowledge network** is a set of interconnected ideas that work together to build knowledge. As students learn new concepts, they build schema—they connect new ideas to existing ones and map them onto a web of knowledge in order to make sense of them and hold them in their memory. Schema grows and changes as students build new knowledge.

Building knowledge is central to reading success. Students are more likely to comprehend what they are reading when the topic is part of their existing schema. Teachers can help students by activating prior knowledge and building background.

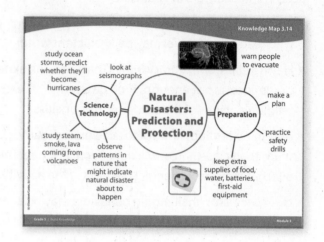

TYPE OF KNOWLEDGE	DEFINITION	**EXAMPLE** *from* Grade 5, Module 3: Natural Disasters
		Essential Question: *How can learning about natural disasters make us safer?*
Prior Knowledge	What students *already know* from prior academic, personal, or cultural experiences	Personal experience may include reading, watching, and listening to media; hearing by word of mouth; or experiencing directly. School experience may include reading books and magazines and viewing websites and other media.
Background Knowledge	What students *need to know* in order to access a topic or concept	Explicit instruction about the topic and genre, the text structure, text and graphic features, media techniques, and content-area vocabulary must be provided.

⬤ *Professional Learning*

RESEARCH FOUNDATIONS

❝ *We must recognize that knowledge is not just accumulating facts; rather, children need to develop knowledge networks, comprised of clusters of concepts that are coherent, generative, and supportive of future learning in a domain.* ❞

—Neuman, Kaefer, & Pinkham (2014)

Building Knowledge in *Into Reading* and *¡Arriba la Lectura!*

Use the Introduce the Topic lessons to build knowledge for each module topic.

- **Access prior knowledge.** At the beginning of each module, use the Introduce the Topic lesson to assess prior knowledge. Use the prompts in the Teacher's Guide to discuss the topic.

- **Build background.** Discuss the module quotation and Essential Question and have students view and discuss the **Get Curious Video** to build knowledge about the topic. Use the **ACTIVE VIEWING** routine to analyze and discuss the video. Use the **VOCABULARY** routine and **Vocabulary Cards** to introduce the module **Big Idea Words**.

- **Teach.** Use the module texts, videos, and vocabulary to teach and discuss key aspects of the topic.

- **Make connections.** Have students continue to build the Knowledge Map in their *myBook* throughout each module. Return to the module **Display and Engage: Knowledge Map** regularly to review, discuss, and connect the topic knowledge students are building.

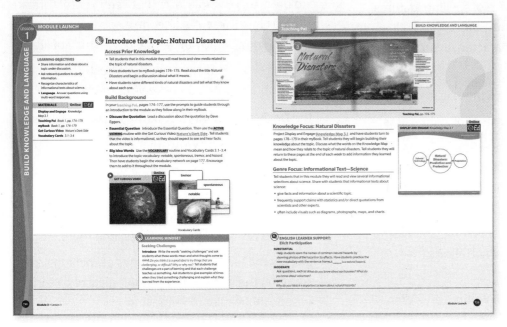

Best Practices: Building Knowledge

Consider these methods for building knowledge.

- **Assess.** Before introducing a topic, ask students what they know about it.

- **Front-load vocabulary.** This is especially important for English learners and others who may not have the language to comprehend topic-based texts or discussions.

- **Make it visual.** Use module **Display and Engage: Knowledge Maps** to discuss with students what they have learned and to help them see how ideas are interconnected.

Developmental Stages of Word Knowledge

Understand how research and students' word knowledge development have informed the sequence of lessons and skills in *Into Reading*.

How Do Students Develop Word Knowledge?

In *Into Reading*, our phonics/decoding and spelling instruction — from the level of foundational skills through the exploration of Latin and Greek word parts —is based on what we know about these stages of developing word knowledge.

There are four stages of word knowledge through which most learners pass in the elementary grades. In Grades 3 through 5, most students will have passed the **Letter-Name/Alphabetic Stage** and be in the **Within Word Pattern** or **Syllables and Affixes Stage**; a few will be in the **Derivational Relationships Stage**. The table on the facing page shows the types and sequence of spelling features learners explore at each of the four stages. Following are the important learner characteristics for each stage in Grades 3 through 5.

At the **Within Word Pattern Stage,** learners

- dramatically increase their store of sight words.

- explore the range of spelling patterns in single-syllable words, and apply this knowledge to decoding two-syllable words and words with simple prefixes and suffixes.

- move toward fluency in their reading, increasing their rate and expression, which allows them to comprehend more fluently.

- become more fluent in their writing, encoding words and ideas more rapidly.

- recognize, or *read*, more words correctly than they will be able to produce, or *spell*, correctly.

- enhance vocabulary through basic morphology — adding prefixes and suffixes to base words.

At the **Syllables and Affixes Stage**, learners

- are able to spell most single-syllable words correctly, which allows them to explore multisyllabic words, applying knowledge of syllable division patterns to spelling and to reading.

- are able to read on-level texts with appropriate fluency.

- write more fluently and extensively.

- develop vocabulary through morphological exploration; the most frequently-occurring Greek and Latin affixes and roots will be introduced and explored: for example *inter* (between) + *rupt* (break) = "break in between" someone else's words; *bio* ("life") + *logy* ("study of ") = biology, "study of life."

- recognize, or *read*, more words correctly than they will be able to produce, or *spell*, correctly.

At the **Derivational Relationships Stage,** learners

- are able to read and write fluently.

- are able to spell most words that they use correctly.

- focus primarily on *vocabulary expansion* by undertaking in-depth exploration of more advanced Latin and Greek prefixes, suffixes, and roots.

- address the few "advanced" types of spelling errors, exploring the meaning/morphological or historical reasons that explain the spelling.

STAGE	DEVELOPMENTAL SPELLINGS	INSTRUCTIONAL FOCUS
Letter-Name/ Alphabetic Beginning Literacy: K to Grade 2	bed – **bad** ship – **shep** float – **fot** drive – **jriv**	• Beginning and ending single consonants • Short vowels • Consonant digraphs (*sh, th*) • Consonant blends (*bl, dr*)
Within Word Pattern Transitional Literacy: Late Grade 1 to Middle of Grade 4	float – **flote** spoil – **spoyle** table – **tabul** chewed – **chood** smudge – **smuge**	• Common long vowel patterns: vowel-consonant-*e*; vowel teams (*ai, oa,* etc.) • *r*- and *l*-influenced vowels • Three-letter consonant blends (*str-, scr-*) • Common spelling for diphthongs /ow/, /oi/ • Complex consonants: final sound of /k/, /ch/, /j/ • Compound words • Homophones: *sail/sale, beat/beet*
Syllables and Affixes Intermediate Literacy: Grades 2 to 6	shopping – **shoping** capture – **capchure** serving – **surving** middle – **middel** fortunate – **forchinet**	• Base words + inflectional endings: *-ed, -ing; -s, -es* • Base words + common prefixes and suffixes • Syllable patterns: VCCV (*bas/ket rab/bit*); VCV open (*hu/man*); VCV closed (*cab/in*) • Less-frequent vowel patterns • Changing final *y* to *i* • Patterns in unaccented syllables • 2-syllable homophones and homographs (*peddle/pedal, dual/duel; PRESent/preSENT; REcord/reCORD*)
Derivational Relationships Skilled/Proficient Literacy: Grades 5 and Up	opposition – **opisition** emphasize – **emphesize** conference – **confrence** commotion – **comotion** feasible – **feasable**	• Spelling/Meaning Relationships: si**g**n music igni**t**e resi**d**e ment**al** si**g**nature musi**c**ian igni**t**ion resi**d**ent ment**al**ity • More advanced exploration of prefixes, suffixes, and Latin and Greek roots • "Absorbed" Prefixes: *in- + mobile =* **im**mobile

Professional Learning

RESEARCH FOUNDATIONS

Children's understanding about how written words "work"—their spelling and how this spelling represents the sounds and meanings of language—is the foundation for reading and writing. This foundation supports children's fluency in word recognition and in writing, and its construction follows a developmental path that can be described in terms of stages of word knowledge.

— Templeton (2011); Templeton & Bear (2018)

Templeton, S. (2011). Teaching spelling in the English/language arts classroom. In Lapp, D., & Fisher, D. (Eds.), *Handbook of Research on Teaching the English Language Arts* (3rd ed.) (pp. 247-251). IRA/NCTE: Erlbaum/Taylor Francis.

Templeton, S., & Bear, D. R. (2018). Word study, research to practice: spelling, phonics, meaning. In D. Lapp & D. Fisher (Eds.), *Handbook of Research on Teaching the English Language Arts* (4th ed.) (pp. 207-232). New York: Routledge/Taylor & Francis.

Teaching and Learning

Decoding and Fluency

Teach students to analyze multisyllabic words, employing their knowledge of phonics to decode increasingly challenging words accurately and fluently.

¡Arriba la Lectura! cuenta con todo esto y más. En la sección ¡Viva el español! verá lo que distingue a este programa.

What Is Decoding?

Decoding is connecting word spellings to their pronunciations. It is the process of translating letters (graphemes) into sounds (phonemes), and then blending the sounds to read words.

Sounds and Letters

In English, there is not always a simple one-to-one correspondence between letters and sounds.

Vowel Digraphs: Two vowels stand for one sound: gr**ai**n, gr**ay**, gr**ea**t, t**ea**ch, n**ee**d, sh**ie**ld, sh**e**.

Silent Letters: Sometimes, two consonants together stand for the sound of one of the letters: **kn**ot, **wr**ap, si**gn**, **rh**yme, and li**mb**.

r-Controlled Vowels: The letter *r* controls the sound of the vowel so that it is neither long nor short: f**er**n, sh**ir**t, c**ur**l, w**or**k.

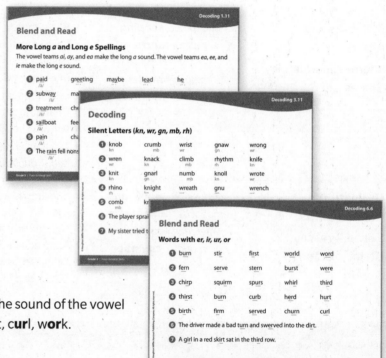

● Professional Learning

RESEARCH FOUNDATIONS

❝ *Phonics [is] an approach to teaching beginning reading that emphasizes letter-sound relationships as the path to efficient word recognition.* ❞

— Cunningham and Zibulsky (2014)

Decoding and Fluency Instruction in *Into Reading* and *¡Arriba la Lectura!*

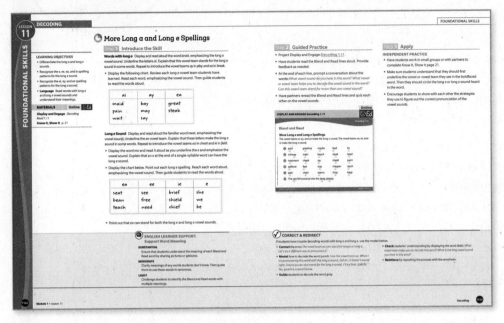

Build students' decoding skills each week.

- The first decoding lesson in each week has students apply the decoding element to shorter words.

- In the second decoding lesson each week, students apply the decoding element to longer multisyllabic words.

- Students use the **Display and Engage: Blend and Read** resources to practice fluency by reading isolated words and words in context.

- Words with the decoding element for the week appear in the multi-paragraph passage on the **Fluency Printable,** giving students another opportunity to read the words in context.

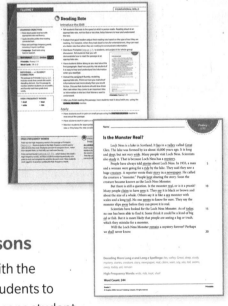

Best Practices: Steps for Teaching Decoding Lessons

- **Introduce the Skill** Provide explicit instruction to read words with the decoding element. Display words with the element and guide students to read them aloud. Point out how the lesson builds on previous lessons student have learned, particularly when students are moving from decoding one- to two-syllable words to decoding multisyllabic words.

- **Guided Practice** Project Display and Engage resources and have students practice reading aloud the Blend and Read lines. Guide them to recognize patterns and to self-correct as they read.

- **Independent Practice** Students use the Know It, Show It resource to practice what they have learned in small groups or with partners.

Teaching and Learning

Spelling

Because of their reciprocal nature, each week's Spelling and Decoding elements are usually connected.

Spelling

Just as **decoding** is the process of translating letters (graphemes) into sounds (phonemes) and then blending to read, **spelling,** or **encoding,** is the reciprocal process of segmenting words into their sounds and representing those sounds (phonemes) with written letters (graphemes).

The research-based resources drawn upon to guide the selection of Spelling Words include extensive word frequency counts of English (Zeno et al., 1996), which inform the most frequently occurring words at each grade level in oral language as well as in print. Through **interactive word sorting,** students discover the features and patterns in Spelling Words, and they apply this understanding efficiently in their reading and writing.

-y	-ey	-ie
silly	alley	brownie
noisy	chimney	pinkie
royalty	attorney	calorie

Spelling Instruction in *Into Reading* and *¡Arriba la Lectura!*

Build skills to master the weekly spelling focus.

Best Practices: Spelling

- **Administer the Pretest** Use the Dictation Sentences Printable and assign Basic, Review, or Challenge Spelling Words accordingly.

- **Teach the Principle** Teach the principle using the Spelling Word Cards Printable as examples.

- **Sort the Words** Work with students to sort the words by spelling pattern and compare the words in each category. Have students practice sorting the words by using copies of the Spelling Word Cards.

- **Reinforce in Small Group** Students use the Proofreading Printable for spelling practice during the week. Reinforce concepts or provide additional practice based on student need.

- **Differentiate Instruction** Support students who are below- or above-level, using **Differentiating Spelling Instruction: Placement Support and Differentiated Lists** in the online Teacher's Guide Additional Resources.

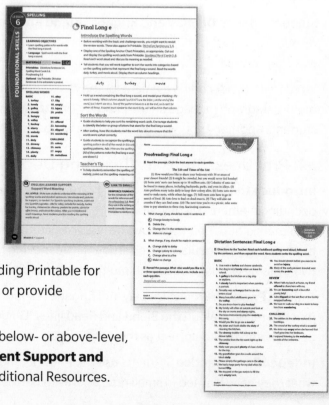

Handwriting and Keyboarding

Handwriting

When students can form letters quickly and easily, the quality and quantity of their writing improves. Instruction for proper grip and paper position for right-handed and left-handed writers, as well as legible letter formation and practice, lead to students' handwriting development.

◉ Professional Learning

RESEARCH FOUNDATIONS

> ❝ *Handwriting is not merely a mechanical, motor skill, but rather a brain-based skill that facilitates meaning-making as writers externalize their cognitions through letter forms, the building blocks of written words and text.* ❞

— Richards et al. (2011)

Use the Handwriting instruction to explain stroke and letter formation, teach writing position, and help students build their handwriting skills. Reproducible models for both manuscript and cursive give students extra support.

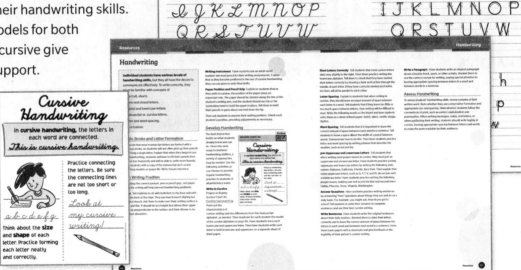

Keyboarding

Keyboarding is a crucial skill for students to learn in order to effectively communicate in writing, create final versions of written assignments and other project materials, and take notes. As students' keyboarding fluency increases, their accuracy and their ability to translate ideas to the screen improve.

Students have an opportunity to practice their keyboarding skills each week by using the Keyboarding Printables in the Literacy Center's Digital Station.

Teaching and Learning

Developing Language and Vocabulary

What Are the Building Blocks of Language?

Language is a symbol system of rule-governed combinations of sounds, words, and sentences that create meaning. **Vocabulary** is the knowledge of words and their meanings—a building block of language. Understanding meaning is more than knowing a word's definition; it also requires an understanding of how the word is constructed and how it functions in relation to other words.

Knowing a Word

To recognize a word in context and use it flexibly, children use what they know about phonology, orthography, morphology, semantics, and syntax.

PHONOLOGY

Understanding the **sounds and pronunciations** of words.

MORPHOLOGY

Using morphemes—or **meaningful word parts** such as base words, prefixes, and suffixes— to understand words.

ORTHOGRAPHY

Understanding the **spelling** of words.

SEMANTICS

Understanding word **meaning** and how it's conveyed by the relationships between words, such as:

* synonyms and antonyms (*fast, quick/slow, fast*)
* shades of meaning (*jog, run, sprint*)
* multiple-meaning words (*bat, ring, wave*)

SYNTAX (grammar)

Understanding the **function** of words and how they relate to each other in a sentence by analyzing:

* the context in which a word is used. Some words only have meaning in sentence context (*and, the, of*)
* the word forms: base words with different suffixes (*walk/walked, hope/hopeful*)
* the word order

● Professional Learning

RESEARCH FOUNDATIONS

❝*Children learn best when words are presented in integrated contexts that make sense to them. A set of words connected to a category such as 'energy' can help children remember not only the words themselves but the linkages in meaning between them.*❞

— Numan & Wright (2014)

Vocabulary in *Into Reading* and *¡Arriba la Lectura!*

The two primary ways that students develop oral language and vocabulary skills are:

Academic Word Instruction

Students learn general academic and domain-specific words using a consistent **VOCABULARY** routine and **Vocabulary Cards.** Instruction focuses on how to pronounce each word, understand its meaning, and use it in context.

Word-Learning Strategies

Vocabulary Strategy and **Generative Vocabulary** lessons help students see the connections between words, deepen their understanding, and provide them with a growing bank of tools to unlock the meanings of unknown words.

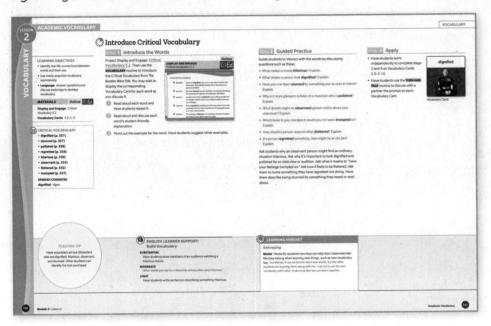

Best Practices: Oral Language and Vocabulary

Create a classroom environment rich in language and vocabulary.

- **Directly teach words.** Use a consistent routine to teach sophisticated words that students will encounter in a variety of texts and across content areas.

- **Address language differences.** Directly teach the language of school and make direct comparisons between "school language" and "home language."

- **Share words in context.** Provide repeated exposures to new words in context. Encourage students to use the words, too.

- **Build curiosity.** Nurture a love for words and an interest in how words work. Brainstorm precise words to replace "tired" word choices in writing.

- **Provide references.** Include print and digital dictionaries, glossaries, and thesauruses in the classroom to support students' word learning.

Engaging Students in Discussion

Students come to school knowing how to listen and speak in social settings, but carefully planned instruction can expand students' listening, speaking, and discussion skills across a variety of contexts.

What Are the Aspects of a Conversation?

Listening and speaking in different contexts means students can transition from informal to formal language, depending on the situation. Students learn intentional listening and speaking skills through direct instruction and purposeful opportunities to hear language modeled in a variety of language situations.

CONTEXT
- *Is the setting formal (in school) or informal (on the playground)?*
- *What language should I use?*

CONTENT
- *What is the conversation about?*
- *What vocabulary do I need to know?*

CUES
- *What social norms are expected? (eye contact, turning toward the speaker)*
- *Am I listening actively?*
- *Are we taking turns?*

Professional Learning

RESEARCH FOUNDATIONS

66 *Students benefit from guidance on how to interact productively in pairs or small groups. Efforts to have students collaborate—perhaps on a research project or in conducting science experiments—easily derail if students do not understand the give-and-take of speaking and listening or the subtle cues of body language in group situations where they work toward a common goal.* 99

—Palmer (2011)

Discussion Skills in *Into Reading* and *¡Arriba la Lectura!*

Discussion skills are developed through listening and speaking instruction. As students become more confident listeners and speakers, they engage in deeper, more meaningful conversations with many practice opportunities. Skills include:

Social Communication

At the beginning of the year, students may practice introducing themselves and others, initiating conversations, following and giving oral directions, and asking for help. Students can also practice taking turns, listening actively, making eye contact, speaking audibly, and learning when to use formal and informal language.

Collaborative Discussion

Students practice collaborative discussion skills by speaking with partners and responding to a discussion question or prompt. Students practice listening for details and ideas from peers and extend conversations by contributing ideas of their own. Students speak clearly and they ask questions to make sure they understand.

Best Practices: Collaborative Discussions

Provide opportunities for students to build and strengthen their listening, speaking, and discussion skills.

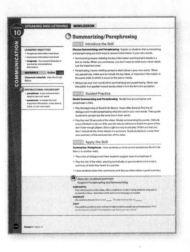

- **Introduce.** Explicitly teach speaking and listening skills. Ask volunteers to help you model a discussion and then have students practice with partners. Be sure to model asking questions for clarification, adding to a conversation, and agreeing or politely disagreeing with peers.

- **Practice.** Build in opportunities for students to practice using listening and speaking skills across all domains. Provide discussion prompts and remind students to use formal language when speaking with partners or in a group.

- **Make it routine.** Use discussion routines, such as **THINK-PAIR-SHARE** and **TURN AND TALK**, to structure conversations between partners.

- **Model appropriate body language.** Remind students to make eye contact, face one another, and listen actively, with their whole bodies.

- **Be sensitive to cultural differences.** Keep in mind that some social norms are not common to all cultures. For example, in some cultures it's a sign of disrespect for students to look an adult in the eye. Others may find it inappropriate to shake hands.

- **Build in informal discussion time.** Encourage students to talk with one another at recess. Acknowledge observations of students using good listening and speaking habits.

Leveraging Text Complexity

Use this table as a reference for text complexity measures and build across the Grade 3 **myBook** texts.

Grade 3 *myBook*

TITLE	AUTHOR	GENRE	LEXILE	GR LEVEL	QUALITATIVE MEASURE
MODULE 1					
Zach Jumps In!		Realistic Fiction	580L		Slightly Complex
Marisol McDonald Doesn't Match	Monica Brown	Realistic Fiction	580L	L	Slightly Complex
Judy Moody, Mood Martian	Megan McDonald	Realistic Fiction	610L	M	Moderately Complex
Stink and the Freaky Frog Freakout	Megan McDonald	Realistic Fiction	570L	M	Slightly Complex
Scaredy Squirrel	Mélanie Watt	Fantasy	630L	L	Moderately Complex
MODULE 2					
A LOL Story		Text/Informal Letter			Slightly Complex
Dear Primo: A Letter to My Cousin	Duncan Tonatiuh	Realistic Fiction/Letters	560L	M	Moderately Complex
Adventures with Words		Poetry	N/A	N/A	Slightly Complex
The Upside Down Boy	Juan Felipe Herrera	Memoir/Narrative Nonfiction	570L	N	Complex
Dear Dragon	Josh Funk	Fantasy/Letters/Poems	550L	E	Slightly Complex
MODULE 3					
American Places, American Ideals		Informational Text with a Map	670L		Complex
The U.S. Constitution	Norman Pearl	Informational Text	650L	P	Moderately Complex
Why We Celebrate the Fourth of July	FreeSchool	Media: Educational Video	N/A	N/A	
The Flag Maker	Susan Campbell Bartoletti	Narrative Nonfiction	620L	R	Complex
Why Is the Statue of Liberty Green?	Martha E. H. Rustad	Narrative Nonfiction	560L	N	Moderately Complex
MODULE 4					
That's Entertainment!		Argument/Opinion Essay	730L		Slightly Complex
The Saga of Pecos Bill	Anthony D. Fredericks	Drama/Tall Tale	N/A	N/A	Slightly Complex
The Traveling Trio: Ceský Krumlov, Czech Republic		Media: Educational Video	N/A	N/A	
Gigi and the Wishing Ring	Adapted from an Italian fairy tale	Drama/Classic Tale	N/A	N/A	Slightly Complex
Two Bear Cubs	Retold by Robert D. San Souci	Drama/Myth	N/A	N/A	Slightly Complex
MODULE 5					
Teamwork = Victory!		Informational Text	700L		Moderately Complex
Soccer Shootout	Jake Maddox and Bob Temple	Realistic Fiction	670L	P	Moderately Complex
Bend It Like Bianca		Media: Humorous Fiction Video	N/A	N/A	
Running Rivals	Jake Maddox	Realistic Fiction	570L	M	Slightly Complex
Brothers at Bat	Audrey Vernick	Narrative Nonfiction	700L	Q	Moderately Complex

TITLE	AUTHOR	GENRE	LEXILE	GR LEVEL	QUALITATIVE MEASURE
MODULE 6					
Frozen Alive		Informational Text	700L		Complex
This Is Your Life Cycle	Heather Lynn Miller	Narrative Nonfiction	700L	N	Moderately Complex
The Nose Awards		Magazine Article/ Informational Text	640L	L	Moderately Complex
Octopus Escapes Again	Laurie Ellen Angus	Narrative Nonfiction	680L	L	Slightly Complex
T.J. the Siberian Tiger Cub	Anne Whitehead Nagda	Informational Text	620L	Q	Complex
MODULE 7					
Let's Build a Park!		Opinion Essay	650L		Slightly Complex
Farmer Will Allen and the Growing Table	Jacqueline Briggs Martin	Biography	650L	T	Moderately Complex
One Plastic Bag	Miranda Paul	Biography	570L	P	Moderately Complex
Energy Island: How One Community Harnessed the Wind and Changed Their World	Allan Drummond	Narrative Nonfiction	770L	P	Moderately Complex
The Storyteller's Candle	Lucía González	Historical Fiction	810L	Q	Moderately Complex
MODULE 8					
A Century of Amazing Inventions		Informational Text	770L		Moderately Complex
Timeless Thomas: How Thomas Edison Changed Our Lives	Gene Barretta	Biography (with informational text)	850L	O	Complex
A Bumpy Ride	Sharon Katz Cooper and Rachel Young	Informational Text	860L	H	Moderately Complex
Rosie Revere, Engineer	Andrea Beaty	Narrative Poetry	780L	Q	Slightly Complex
Edison's Best Invention		Opinion Text	850L	U	Complex
MODULE 9					
Great Ideas from Great Parents!		Editorial	760L		Slightly Complex
How Did That Get in My Lunchbox?	Chris Butterworth	Informational Text	880L	O	Complex
Carrots, Farm to Fork		Media: Educational Video	N/A	N/A	
How Do You Raise a Raisin?	Pam Muñoz Ryan	Informational Text (with poetry)	860L	T	Complex
It's Our Garden: From Seeds to Harvest in a School Garden		Informational Text	640L	N	Moderately Complex
MODULE 10					
Why We Share Stories		Informational Text/ Article	800L		
When the Giant Stirred	Celia Godkin	Legend	980L	S	Complex
Why the Sky Is Far Away	Marcy Stillerman	Folktale	790L	R	Moderately Complex
Cinder Al and the Stinky Footwear	Roger Lore	Fairy Tale	870L	S	Complex
Compay Mono and Comay Jicotea	Retold by Joe Hayes	Folktale	670L	U	Complex

CONTENT CONNECTIONS | Science Connections | Social Studies Connections | Language Arts | Art & Music

Teaching and Learning

Leveraging Text Complexity

Use this table as a reference for text complexity measures and build for the Grade 4 *myBook* texts.

Grade 4 *myBook*

TITLE	AUTHOR	GENRE	LEXILE	GR LEVEL	QUALITATIVE MEASURE
MODULE 1					
The Story of You		Photo Essay	660L		Slightly Complex
Flora and Ulysses: The Illuminated Adventures	Kate DiCamillo	Fantasy	560L	W	Moderately Complex
Yes! We Are Latinos!	Alma Flor Ada and F. Isabel Campoy	Narrative Poetry		L	Slightly Complex
The Year of the Rat	Grace Lin	Realistic Fiction	630L	O	Moderately Complex
Kitoto the Mighty	Tololwa M. Mollel	Folktale	610L	V	Slightly Complex
MODULE 2					
What Are the Five Senses?		Infographic	900L		Moderately Complex
The Science Behind Sight	Louis Spilsbury	Informational Text	600L	K	Moderately Complex
Animal Senses	from *Animal Atlas*	Informational Video	N/A		Slightly Complex
Blind Ambition	Matthew Cooper as told to Rachel Buchholtz	Personal Narrative	750L	J	Slightly Complex
The Game of Silence	Louise Erdrich	Historical Fiction	770L	K	Moderately Complex
MODULE 3					
Never Give Up!	Louise Erdrich	Argumentative Text	770L		Moderately Complex
Rent Party Jazz	William Miller	Historical Fiction	820L	Q	Slightly Complex
The Galveston Hurricane of 1900		Narrative Nonfiction	940L	R	Moderately Complex
Catch Me If You Can	Carol Schaffner	Play	N/A	M	Moderately Complex
My Diary from Here to There	Amada Irma Pérez	Diary/Autobiographical Fiction	780L	P	Slightly Complex
MODULE 4					
Who's a Hero?		Informational Text	840L		Moderately Complex
Prince Charming Misplaces His Bride	Christopher Healy	Fairy Tale	810L	V	Moderately Complex
Smokejumpers to the Rescue!	Laurie Toupin	Informational Text	790L	T	Moderately Complex
Perseus and the Fall of Medusa	Claire Daniel	Myth/Play	N/A	T	Moderately Complex
The Battle of the Alamo	Amie Jane Leavitt	Narrative Nonfiction	700L	Y	Complex
MODULE 5					
Why Art Centers Matter		Argumentative Text	890L		Moderately Complex
The Beatles Were Fab (and They Were Funny)	Kathleen Krull and Paul Brewer	Biography	860L	X	Moderately Complex
How Can Photos Take Us Back in Time?	from The Metropolitan Museum of Art #MetKids	Video	N/A		Moderately Complex
Let's Dance Around the World	Leticia Ann Kimura and Annabel Wildrick	Informational Text	970L	S	Moderately Complex
The Art of Poetry	J. Patrick Lewis, Bob Raczka, Henry Wadsworth Longfellow, and Francisco X. Alarcón	Poetry	N/A		Moderately Complex

TITLE	AUTHOR	GENRE	LEXILE	GR LEVEL	QUALITATIVE MEASURE
MODULE 6					
Seven Natural Wonders		Informational Text	900L		Moderately Complex
Mariana Trench	Michael Woods and Mary B. Woods	Informational Text	890L	S	Complex
Weird and Wondrous Rocks	April Pulley Sayre	Informational Text	870L	S	Moderately Complex
Nature's Wonders	Robert Schechter, X.J. Kennedy, Carol R. Baik, and Steven Withrow	Poetry and Informational Text	1010L	Q	Complex
Grand Canyon: A Trail Through Time	Linda Vieira	Literary Nonfiction	1140L	T	Complex
MODULE 7					
A Tale of Traditional Tales		Informational Text	920L		Moderately Complex
Thunder Rose	Jerdine Nolan	Tall Tale	910L	T	Moderately Complex
In the Days of King Adobe	Joe Hayes	Folktale	660L	L	Slightly Complex
A Pair of Tricksters	Aesop, John and Caitlin Matthews	Fable/Trickster Tale	670L	J	Slightly Complex
Ten Suns: A Chinese Legend and The Ten Suns	Retold by Eric A. Kimmel; directed by Oded Levy	Legend and Video	770L	L	Moderately Complex
MODULE 8					
To Your Health!		Informational Text	970L		Moderately Complex
Eco-Friendly Food	Cath Senker	Informational/ Argumentative Text	950L	K	Complex
Kids Rock Nutrition in the Kitchen	from Nutrition.gov	Video	N/A		Moderately Complex
Bug Bites		Informational Text	900L	L	Complex
Now You're Cooking!	René Saldaña, Jr.	Realistic Fiction/ Recipe	750L	K	Moderately Complex
MODULE 9					
The Eco Guardians		Letters	840L		Moderately Complex
Luz Sees the Light	Claudia Dávila	Graphic Novel	800L	I	Moderately Complex
On Sea Turtle Patrol and Saving the Kemp's Ridley Sea Turtle	Nancy Dawson; from Texas Parks and Wildlife	Realistic Fiction and Informational Video	840L	M	Moderately Complex
How Can We Reduce Household Waste?	Mary K. Pratt	Informational/ Argumentative Text	790L	K	Complex
Seeds of Change	Jen Cullerton Johnson	Biography	800L	M	Moderately Complex
MODULE 10					
How Technology Has Changed Communication		Timeline	880L		Complex
The History of Communication		Informational Text	1070L	N	Complex
A New Language—Invented by Kids!	Charnan Simon	Narrative Nonfiction	850L	L	Moderately Complex
Dolphin Dinner	from National Geographic Kids.com	Informational Video	N/A		Moderately Complex
Cooper's Lesson	Sun Yung Shin	Realistic Fiction	630L	O	Moderately Complex

CONTENT CONNECTIONS | Science Connections | Social Studies Connections | Language Arts | Art & Music

Teaching and Learning

Leveraging Text Complexity

Use this table as a reference for text complexity measures and build for the Grade 5 **myBook** texts.

Grade 5 myBook

TITLE	AUTHOR	GENRE	LEXILE	GR LEVEL	QUALITATIVE MEASURE
MODULE 1					
Government Must Fund Inventors		Persuasive Essay	870L		Slightly Complex
The Inventor's Secret: What Thomas Edison Told Henry Ford	Suzanne Slade and Jennifer Black Reinhardt	Narrative Nonfiction	710L	S	Slightly Complex
Winds of Hope	Katy Duffield	Narrative Nonfiction	1020L	V	Moderately Complex
Wheelchair Sports: Hang Glider to Wheeler-Dealer	Simon Shapiro	Informational Text	930L	V	Slightly Complex
Captain Arsenio: Inventions and (Mis)Adventures in Flight	Pablo Bernasconi	Science Fiction/Fantasy	900L	T	Slightly Complex
MODULE 2					
Many Ways to Tell a Story		Informational Text	1060L		Slightly Complex
Airborn	Kenneth Oppel	Fantasy/Adventure	820L	V	Moderately Complex
The Secret Garden	Frances Hodgson Burnett	Fantasy	800L	V	Slightly Complex
The Miracle of Spring	Helen Hanna	Play	N/A	N/A	Moderately Complex
The Poem That Will Not End: Fun with Poetic Forms and Voices	Joan Bransfield Graham	Poetry	N/A	N/A	Moderately Complex
MODULE 3					
Who Studies Natural Disasters?		Friendly Letter	850L		Moderately Complex
Eruption! Volcanoes and the Science of Saving Lives	Elizabeth Rusch	Narrative Nonfiction	870L	X	Moderately Complex
Between the Glacier and the Sea: The Alaska Earthquake	The Valdez Museum	Media: Video	N/A	N/A	N/A
Quaking Earth, Racing Waves	Rachel Young	Informational Text	1060L	Y	Moderately Complex
Hurricanes: The Science Behind Killer Storms	Alvin and Virginia Silverstein and Laura Silverstein Nunn	Informational Text	920L	U	Moderately Complex
MODULE 4					
Why Go West?		Informational Text	840L		Slightly Complex
Explore the Wild West!	Anita Yasuda	Informational Text	910L	W	Moderately Complex
The Celestials' Railroad	Bruce Watson	Informational Text	1020L	W	Moderately Complex
Homesteading	Prairie Public Broadcasting	Media: Video	N/A	N/A	N/A
A Pioneer Sampler: The Daily Life of a Pioneer Family in 1840	Barbara Greenwood	Historical Fiction	860L	Q	Moderately Complex
MODULE 5					
The Protective Power of Nature Preserves		Informational Text	940L		Slightly Complex
Potatoes on Rooftops: Farming in the City	Hadley Dyer	Persuasive Text	1020L	S	Moderately Complex
Living Green	Doreen Beauergard	Play	N/A	N/A	Slightly Complex
The Good Garden: How One Family Went from Hunger to Having Enough	Katie Smith Milway	Realistic Fiction	620L	O	Slightly Complex
Parrots Over Puerto Rico	Susan L. Roth and Cindy Trumbore	Informational Text	850L	Q	Moderately Complex

TITLE	AUTHOR	GENRE	LEXILE	GR LEVEL	QUALITATIVE MEASURE
MODULE 6					
Let's Get Creative	N/A	Infographic	930L	N/A	Moderately Complex
Christo and Jeanne-Claude: Through the Gates and Beyond	Jan Greenberg and Sandra Jordan	Informational Text	1010L	W	Complex
Rita Moreno	Juan Felipe Herrera	Biography	1020L	U	Complex
Play, Louis, Play! The True Story of a Boy and His Horn	Muriel Harris Weinstein	Fictionalized Biography	860L	U	Moderately Complex
Phillis's Big Test	Catherine Clinton	Biography	980L	T	Moderately Complex
MODULE 7					
A Few Who Dared		Mini-Biographies	1090L		Moderately Complex
Into the Unknown: Above and Below	Stewart Ross	Informational Text	1040L	Y	Complex
Great Discoveries and Amazing Adventures: Stories of Hidden Marvels and Lost Treasures	Claire Llewellyn	Informational Text	1020L	W	Complex
SpaceShipOne	Matthew Stinemetze (as told to Naomi Wallace)	Autobiography	950L	Y	Moderately Complex
The Mighty Mars Rovers: The Incredible Adventures of Spirit and Opportunity	Elizabeth Rusch	Narrative Nonfiction	950L	X	Moderately Complex
MODULE 8					
Moving to a New Country: A Survival Guide		Informational Text/ Guide	900L		Slightly Complex
A Movie In My Pillow	Jorge Argueta	Poetry	N/A	N/A	Moderately Complex
From Scratch	Susie Castellano	Realistic Fiction	960L	U	Moderately Complex
Elisa's Diary	Doris Luisa Oronoz	Realistic Fiction	800L	T	Moderately Complex
Inside Out and Back Again	Thanhha Lai	Poetry	N/A	N/A	Complex
MODULE 9					
Why People Love Mysteries		Informational Text	1070L		Moderately Complex
Mr. Linden's Library	Walter Dean Myers	Mystery	990L	Y	Complex
The Loch Ness Monster	National Geographic	Media: Video	N/A	N/A	N/A
Finding Bigfoot: Everything You Need to Know	Martha Brockenbrough	Informational/ Persuasive Text	1050L	Z	Complex
The Secret Keepers	Trenton Lee Stewart	Mystery	720L	V	Moderately Complex
MODULE 10					
Why We Watch Animals		Informational Text	990L		Moderately Complex
Willie B.: A Story of Hope	Nancy Roe Pimm	Narrative Nonfiction	1020L	T	Complex
Dolphin Parenting	National Geographic	Media: Video	N/A	N/A	
Can We Be Friends?	Ellen R. Braaf	Informational Text	1040L	T	Complex
Winter Bees and Other Poems of the Cold	Joyce Sidman	Multigenre Text (Poetry/ Informational)		S	Complex

CONTENT CONNECTIONS   Science Connections   Social Studies Connections   Language Arts   Art & Music

Teaching and Learning

Teaching with Text Sets

Help students build and deepen their knowledge of specific topics through reading and discussing multi-genre text sets.

What Are Text Sets?

Text sets are collections of texts focused on a specific topic. When students read multiple texts on a topic, their understanding of that topic deepens, and they can use knowledge gained from reading one text to help them understand the next one, increasing their topic knowledge and vocabulary.

- Text sets are effective for building knowledge and vocabulary and for preparing students to read new texts about the same topic.

- Text sets provide background knowledge that helps readers make inferences, which aids comprehension and memory.

- Text sets provide a means of focused study beyond the content of a single text. Readers begin to think more critically and analytically because they have deepened their knowledge about a topic by reading multiple texts.

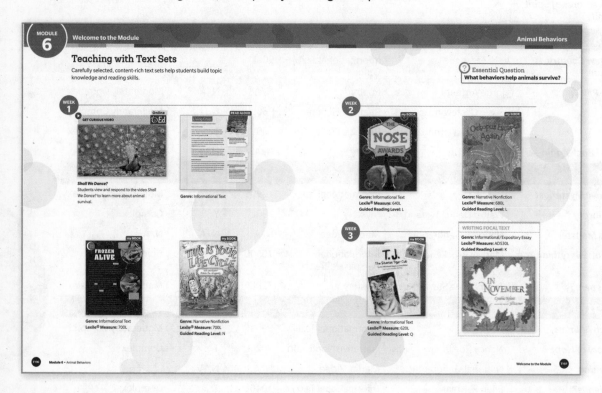

Teaching with Text Sets in *Into Reading* and *¡Arriba la lectura!*

Each module in *Into Reading* and *¡Arriba la lectura!* consists of a curated multi-genre collection of texts around a single topic. The texts for each module are carefully grouped in a way that contributes to students' genre and content knowledge through the use of these features:

• a **Get Curious** video to spark interest in the topic

• an Essential Question, addressed in each module text, to inspire inquiry and to set a purpose for reading

• a short text to activate background knowledge and build schema for the topic

• a topical text read aloud by the teacher to model fluent reading and to promote listening comprehension

• the **myBook** interactive student text in which students take notes and annotate the text in order to cite text evidence

• a trade book used as a model for Writer's Workshop lessons as well as for book club discussion groups

Best Practices: Teaching with Text Sets

• **Establish a purpose.** Use the Essential Question to guide students' work through the text set. Give students a purpose for reading each of the texts, such as using knowledge of the genre to make predictions about the content, noting the way an author organizes information, or stating what they would like to learn from the text.

• **Note similarities and differences between texts.** Help students compare the various ways that the topic is addressed by the different authors in the module and how information in one text can contribute to students' understanding of another text and of the topic itself.

• **Model making connections.** Support students as they begin reading and thinking across texts. For example, collaborate to build and discuss a Knowledge Map that shows what students have learned about the topic.

• **Facilitate discussion.** Model and provide opportunities for students to share responses to each text in the module and to participate in collaborative discussion of the topic and the texts.

Shared Reading

Teach comprehension and literary analysis skills in Reading Workshop lessons and develop oral language skills through shared reading and discussion of **myBook** texts.

What Is Shared Reading?

Shared reading is an interactive experience in which students join in the reading of a text as prompted by the teacher. Students have the opportunity to practice and apply comprehension skills and strategies, literary analysis, speaking and listening, and response to texts, using the Reading Workshop model.

Minilessons on a target skill or strategy in the Teacher's Guide set the stage for the day's lesson and provide a focus for the community shared reading experience of the **myBook** texts. For the teacher, the **Teaching Pal** contains all the **myBook** texts with color-coded point-of-use questions and prompts to guide students' critical thinking and text analysis.

READ FOR UNDERSTANDING
During a first reading, use questions and prompts to help students **get the gist of the text.**

Notice & Note
Use these notes to help students **recognize Signposts** that alert readers to significant moments in the text and help readers create meaning.

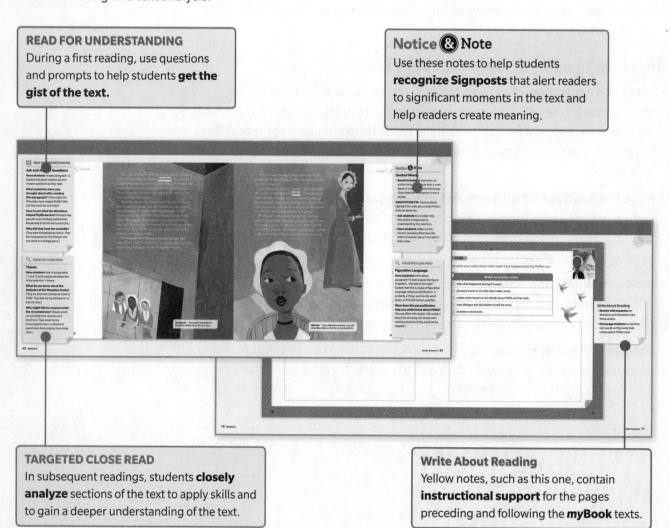

TARGETED CLOSE READ
In subsequent readings, students **closely analyze** sections of the text to apply skills and to gain a deeper understanding of the text.

Write About Reading
Yellow notes, such as this one, contain **instructional support** for the pages preceding and following the **myBook** texts.

Shared Reading in *Into Reading* and *¡Arriba la Lectura!*

Shared reading lessons provide the tools to help students grow as readers, writers, and critical thinkers as they read texts together.

- Minilessons in the Teacher's Guide before reading provide instruction in skills and strategies through the use of highly visual **Anchor Charts** that help focus students' thinking and serve as reminders during and after reading.

- Use the **Teaching Pal** for:

  » **First readings.** The blue Read for Understanding notes in the **Teaching Pal** guide students' understanding of the text through purpose-setting, think-aloud strategy modeling, and text-based questions with annotation tips to promote active reading.

  » **Strategies for close reading.** Promote deeper thinking about and understanding of texts using the Notice & Note support. Red notes in the **Teaching Pal** support students as they identify and use Signposts in the text to create meaning.

  » **Targeted close reading.** The purple notes identify opportunities for students to apply skills and demonstrate knowledge when revisiting specific sections of the text during rereading.

  » **Responding to texts.** Yellow notes provide instructional support for the pre- and post-reading pages. These include guidance for academic discussion, response writing, and completing performance tasks.

Best Practices: Shared Reading

Use the suggestions below when you read with your class.

- Demonstrate behaviors of fluent and analytical readers, such as reading with expression and using think-alouds for modeling.

- When students respond to questions or share ideas, ask them to support their thinking with evidence from the text.

- Prompt students to listen to and respond to each other. Remind them that they can develop fuller understanding when they have the benefit of others' interpretations.

- Use a gradual release model in which you teach a minilesson about a target skill or strategy, guide students to apply it to a common text, and have students practice independently through oral or written response activities.

Close Reading

Build students' reading comprehension through the close reading of texts.

What Is Close Reading?

Close reading involves the reading and rereading of text to more deeply understand it. In close reading:

- readers use prior knowledge to examine both explicit and implicit meaning in the text.

- readers interact with the text to make logical inferences, to note how the text is constructed, and to recognize and understand the choices the author made.

- readers use text evidence to support their conclusions and thoughts in order to reach a deeper understanding of the text's meaning.

Close Reading in *Into Reading* and *¡Arriba la Lectura!*

The write-in student **myBook** is designed to help students grow as readers and writers. Guided by the teacher notes in the **Teaching Pal**, students reread specific sections of their **myBook** texts to apply skills. Students annotate the text to demonstrate their thinking and support their understanding. Students look for specific evidence in the text to support their understanding of the following:

- text structure and organization
- text and graphic features
- literary elements
- central idea

- ideas and support
- theme
- point of view
- figurative language and other literary devices

After reading, students engage in collaborative discussion to answer questions about the text. Students also use text evidence to respond in writing to prompts in the **myBook**.

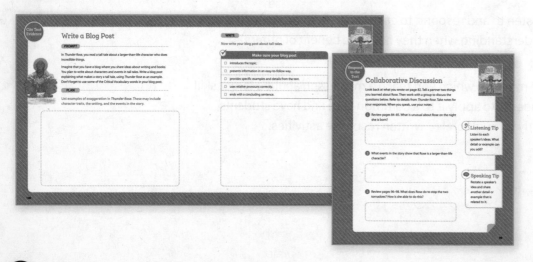

Using Notice & Note Signposts

Notice & Note Signposts help students think more deeply about the texts they read. Through introduction of the Signposts in the **Teacher's Guide** and through guided support in the **Teaching Pal**, students learn how to recognize each signpost in the text, pause in their reading to ask key questions, and then look for the answers using clues in the text.

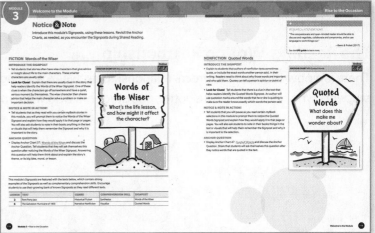

Signposts for works of fiction include:

- **Contrasts & Contradictions:** sharp contrasts between what readers expect will happen and what a character actually says or does

- **Words of the Wiser:** the advice or insights that a wiser, usually older, character offers to the main character; these life lessons provide insights into the theme of the text

- **Aha Moment:** the moment when a character reaches a realization about something that shifts his or her actions or understandings

- **Again & Again:** recurring events, images, or words and phrases in the text that may signal symbolism, character development, or theme

- **Memory Moment:** when a character shares a memory that interrupts the story progression

- **Tough Questions:** difficult questions a character asks himself or herself that reveal the character's internal conflict

Signposts for works of nonfiction include:

- **Contrasts & Contradictions:** contrasts and contradictions within the text and between the text and the reader's own knowledge and experience

- **Extreme and Absolute Language:** language that seems to exaggerate or overstate a claim by attempting to leave no doubt in the reader's mind

- **Numbers and Stats:** numbers, statistics, and language an author uses to either provide precision or to avoid it

- **Quoted Words:** language an author uses to support a point, either through a direct quotation or through a summary or paraphrase of the written or spoken words

- **Word Gaps:** vocabulary that may be unfamiliar to readers, such as technical language, discipline-specific vocabulary, or rare words

- **3 Big Questions:** readers may challenge an author's assertions when they conflict with prior knowledge, in order to separate fact from opinion

Reading-Writing Connections

Make frequent connections while teaching to reinforce the reciprocal relationship between reading and writing.

The Reading-Writing Relationship

There is a powerful and reciprocal relationship between reading and writing—students who read more write better, and students who write more read better.

I Can Read!

READING IMPACTS WRITING

- Reading builds background knowledge to use in writing.
- Decoding knowledge in reading supports spelling in writing.
- Reading expands vocabulary that can be used in writing.
- Reading across genres supports writing in a variety of genres.
- Analyzing and discussing texts support organization, voice, and word choice in writing.

WRITING IMPACTS READING

- Writing provides an authentic purpose and audience for reading.
- Writing in response to reading deepens reading comprehension.
- Sharing writing with peers and reading aloud build reading fluency.

I Can Write!

Writing to Sources

Build strong connections between reading and writing by using writing tasks that are embedded throughout *Into Reading* and *¡Arriba la Lectura!*

Following each main text in **myBook**, students respond to their reading through a **Write About Reading** task. Each task includes a writing prompt, planning space with a graphic organizer, and space to write, including reminders to go back into the text to cite text evidence. Over the course of the year, students write in a wide variety of modes and forms.

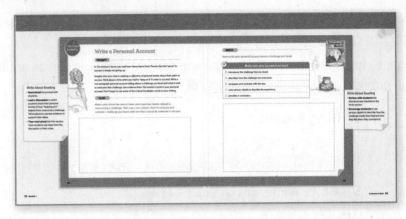

Performance Tasks

At the end of each module, students complete a **Performance Task** writing assignment based on the module's Essential Question. The prompt asks students to synthesize at least two texts from the module in order to complete the task. Students use graphic organizers in their **myBook** to plan and draft their writing. A checklist for revising and editing reminds students to review their work and correct it, as needed. Finally, students create a finished copy of their writing to share with others.

Students may complete these writing tasks during independent work time. Use the yellow notes in the **Teaching Pal** to scaffold support, as needed.

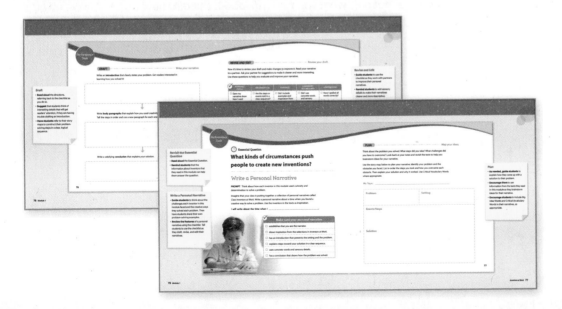

Teaching and Learning

Teaching Writing as a Process

When students learn, practice, and internalize a step-by-step plan for writing, they become efficient at turning ideas into published writing products.

Stages of the Writing Process

Engage students in the writing process to generate ideas, organize drafts, revise, edit, publish, and share a wide variety of texts.

The Writing Process

- PREWRITE: Choose a topic and organize your ideas.
- DRAFT: Write down your ideas.
- REVISE: Improve the ideas, organization, and style of your writing.
- EDIT: Correct errors in grammar, spelling, and punctuation.
- PUBLISH/SHARE: Finalize and share your completed work with others.

● Professional Learning

RESEARCH FOUNDATIONS

66 *The writing process is a learned skill. It comes from many hours spent writing a lot. It comes from a mindset that whatever you write, you consider not only what you will write about but also how you will write well.* 99

—Calkins & Ehrenworth (2016)

Writing Process in *Into Reading* and *¡Arriba la Lectura!*

Use the **Writing Workshop Teacher's Guide** lessons to provide explicit modeling and instruction for each stage of the writing process. In each Writing Workshop module, students focus on a particular writing mode and explore it through all stages of the writing process.

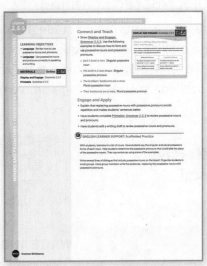

- Each writing module is tied to a **Focal Text**—an authentic trade book used as a mentor text for the mode.

- Students write daily, set their own writing goals, and confer regularly with teachers and peers.

- Through the use of instructional tools such as **Anchor Charts** and **Display & Engage** content, as well as the modeling in the **Focal Texts**, students find the keys to unlock the love of writing.

- Plan time to write every day, starting with shorter sessions initially, and gradually build students' writing stamina through the year.

- Allow for flexibility in the writing process, acknowledging that students will often be at different stages of the process and supporting them accordingly.

- Offer choice whenever possible—in materials for writing, flexible seating for independent writing, and topics for writing. For example, use writing prompts as a starting point, knowing that they may help some students get their ideas flowing, while others may respond well to having more choice.

Best Practices: Grammar Through Writing

Grammar, language, and conventions are taught most effectively in the context of authentic writing instruction, in the moment when a new skill or concept is most useful to students. The **Writing Workshop Teacher's Guide** provides multiple paths for Grammar instruction which you may use flexibly to best serve your students' needs.

- **Integrated** Use the Targeted Grammar Support suggestions at point-of-use in the revising and editing steps of the writing process.

- **Differentiated** Choose from the bank of Grammar Minilessons in the back of your **Writing Workshop Teacher's Guide** to provide targeted support for students who need something different than the integrated grammar lesson.

- **Systematic** For a systematic grammar scope and sequence, follow the recommended path on the Week at a Glance pages in the **Writing Workshop Teacher's Guide**.

Facilitating Inquiry and Research Projects

Engage students in projects that provide opportunities to extend content knowledge while building research, writing, listening, speaking, and collaboration skills.

What Is Project-Based Learning?

Inquiry and research projects require students to work for an extended period of time to solve a problem, answer a question, or share information. Projects are most effective when they allow students to explore their interests or have real-world applications, such as solving a problem in the community.

Steps for Effective Project-Based Learning

STEP 3

PRESENT AND REFLECT
Students **share** what they learned with their audience.

STEP 2

WRITE AND CREATE
Students write, build, create, and **work toward** their project **goal.**

STEP 1

LAUNCH THE PROJECT
Connect the project to a topic or skill students are learning. Establish a real-world **purpose** and **audience** for the project. Students **generate research questions** and **develop a research plan.**

Professional Learning

RESEARCH FOUNDATIONS

66 *When learners have a compelling purpose to achieve and a meaningful audience to reach, we see their attention to tasks, their willingness to persevere in reading challenging texts, and even their motivation to revise and edit their work increase. In fact, people seem to be built for learning through projects.* 99

— Duke (2015)

Inquiry and Research in *Into Reading* and *¡Arriba la lectura!*

Students work on a three-week Inquiry and Research Project per module. Student groups use a Project Printable each week to work independently through the project steps, building decision-making and problem-solving skills in the process.

- **Week 1: Brainstorm and Research** Launch the project and make connections to the module topic. Then have students collaborate to generate research questions, develop a research plan, and explore an area of curiosity about the topic. Provide support for research skills as needed. Make available source material, including books, student magazines, videos, and online resources, or guide students to set up in-person interviews and exploratory visits to gather relevant information.

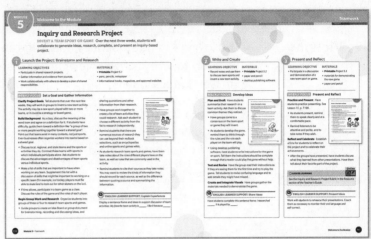

- **Week 2: Write and Create** Give students time for drafting and revising their work. Provide materials appropriate to the project, including a variety of writing and art supplies, sources of visuals, and software, if available.

- **Week 3: Present and Reflect** Have students practice their presentation skills before sharing their final product with an audience. Assess project work using the **Inquiry and Research Project Rubric** in the Resources section of the Teacher's Guide. Be sure to celebrate students' hard work.

Best Practices: Facilitating Inquiry and Research Projects

- **Identify a real-world problem or question.** Have students brainstorm how to solve a real problem, answer a question, or address a need in their own life, school, or community.

- **Select an outside audience.** Provide opportunities for students to share their work with another class, family members, local business owners, or community members.

- **Schedule project work.** Select a time when students will work on their projects each week, such as during Literacy Center rotations.

- **Build research skills.** Model how to find and record information, including how to conduct an interview and how to make and record observations.

- **Allow time for revision.** Build in time for students to revise and finalize their final products. Provide feedback as needed.

- **Support English learners.** Allow English learners to participate at their language levels. Consider sharing written sources and providing samples of the final product in students' home language.

Teaching with Instructional Routines

Instructional Routines at a Glance

Into Reading and *¡Arriba la Lectura!* include support and suggestions for using these instructional routines.

ROUTINE	PURPOSE	ROUTINE IN ACTION
Active Viewing	Build and extend students' knowledge about the module topic by actively viewing and responding to Get Curious Videos.	Grade 3, 4, 5 Teacher's Guide, Volume 1, p. T15
Vocabulary	Explicitly teach the meaning of general academic and domain-specific words, provide examples, and practice using the words in context.	Grade 3, 4, 5 Teacher's Guide, Volume 1, p. T205
Active Listening	Increase students' familiarity with fluent reading and develop their listening comprehension through active listening and responding to text read aloud.	Grade 3, 4, 5 Teacher's Guide, Volume 2, p. T15
Read for Understanding	Develop students' reading comprehension of a full text by setting a purpose before reading, monitoring comprehension during reading, and summarizing or retelling after reading.	Grade 3, 4, 5 Teacher's Guide, Volume 2, p. T205
Collaborative Discussion	Build students' facility in group discussion with recalling, retelling, or summarizing key ideas in text and supporting responses by citing text evidence.	Grade 3, 4, 5 Teacher's Guide, Volume 3, p. T15
Close Reading	Build students' ability to analyze text closely by rereading and annotating, citing text evidence, and applying reading skills and strategies.	Grade 3, 4, 5 Teacher's Guide, Volume 3, p. T205
Response Writing	Build students' ability to cite evidence when writing in response to texts and other selections.	Grade 3, 4, 5 Teacher's Guide, Volume 4, p. T15
Turn and Talk	Foster peer interaction through positive discussion habits and provide scaffolding for students to take ownership of their learning.	Grade 3, 4, 5 Teacher's Guide, Volume 4, p. T205
Think-Pair-Share	Promote participation in classroom discussion by providing a structure in which all students can demonstrate higher-level thinking skills.	Grade 3, 4, 5 Teacher's Guide, Volume 5, p. T15
Partner Reading	Build students' independence and accountability through fluency practice as partners apply decoding skills when reading connected text..	Grade 3, 4, 5 Teacher's Guide, Volume 5, p. T205

KEY ■ Build Knowledge and Language ■ Communication ■ Reading ■ Vocabulary

Embedded Instructional Routines

Instructional routines are embedded in *Into Reading* lessons to target the acquisition of key skills and to build structure and continuity between lessons.

Look for instructional routines highlighted in **GREEN** throughout the lessons in the Teacher's Guide.

Preview the consistent routine steps and model language before teaching a lesson.

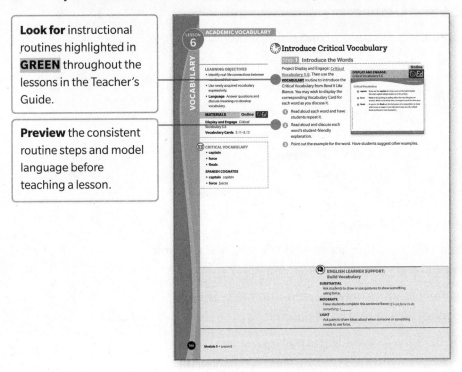

Take a Deep Dive

Each module in the Teacher's Guide spotlights one of the routines.

Learn why the routine is important and how it helps students develop their literacy skills.

Access suggestions for using *Into Reading* materials to teach the routine.

Examine the consistent set of steps and model language for teaching the routine.

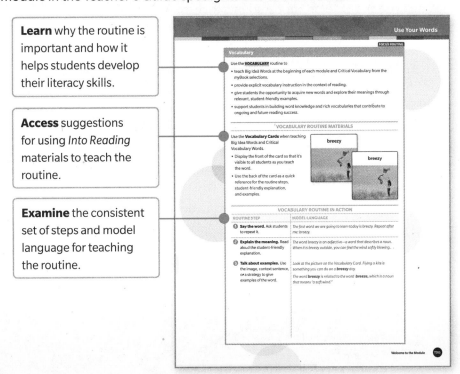

Teaching and Learning

Engaging Students in Learning

Use routines to strategically structure student engagement so that all students are actively participating, thinking, and responding.

Engagement Routines at a Glance

Into Reading and *¡Arriba la Lectura!* include support and suggestions for using the following engagement routines.

GRADES 3–5 ENGAGEMENT ROUTINES	
• Choral Reading	• Turn and Talk
• Partner Reading	• Think-Pair-Share
• Echo Reading	• Solo Chair

Everyone Talking, Everyone Learning

Remember these key points for creating a safe environment in which all students feel comfortable participating and engaging in their learning.

• Model and practice engagement routines until they are automatic. Show examples (and non-examples) of how to be a good partner.

• Provide thinking time for all students to consider responses.

• Use consistent nonverbal signals to let students know when it's time to think or respond. For example, raise your hand to signal thinking time and lower it to signal response time.

• Check for participation by making eye contact to prompt students to respond or to remind the group that you expect everyone to respond.

Professional Learning

RESEARCH FOUNDATIONS

66 *Master teachers create an active-learning environment in which students are on task in their thinking and speaking or are collaboratively working close to 100 percent of the time. Such teachers notice and measure not only when students are on task but also the quality of their engagement.* 99

— de Frondeville (2009)

ECHO READING

ECHO READING is an oral reading routine in which the teacher reads aloud phrase-by-phrase and students repeat each phrase. Use this routine for reading directions, books with one or two sentences per page, or short lines of a shared text.

ROUTINE IN ACTION

1 Read along.

- Display a book, short text, or directions.
- Tell students to listen as you read aloud one sentence at a time.
- Ask students to listen carefully as you model fluent reading.

2 Repeat together.

- Ask students to "echo" you, imitating your pronunciation and expression. *Let's pretend we're in a cave and you all are my echo. So, when I pause, everyone repeats what I read at the same time.*
- Read aloud the text, pointing to the words and pausing at natural intervals for students to chorally repeat each sentence or phrase.
- Check for participation. Make eye contact with students who are not repeating or stop to cue the whole group.

CHORAL READING

CHORAL READING engages students with reading aloud a text multiple times in a group setting. Use this routine with small chunks of text, short lines of shared or familiar text, and procedures or directions.

ROUTINE IN ACTION

1 Read along with a text.

- Display a short text or provide copies and ask students to follow along silently as you read aloud the entire text. Have students listen as you model fluent reading with appropriate expression, pacing, and rate.

2 Read aloud together.

- Tell students that everyone will read together, starting at the same time and reading at the same rate.

3 Listen as you read.

- Check for participation. If students read at different rates, remind them that the goal is to sound like one voice.

PARTNER READING

PARTNER READING engages pairs of students in reading a familiar text multiple times. Use this routine to reread texts students have already read with teacher guidance.

ROUTINE IN ACTION

1 Partner up.

- Pair students and assign numbers (1/2), and make sure partners remember their numbers.

2 Take turns reading.

- Tell partners who will read first and how much of the text to read. For example, Partner 1 reads first, while Partner 2 listens and follows along. Then partners switch roles.

3 Read the text.

- Have students reread the text, with the other partner reading first.

TURN AND TALK

TURN AND TALK is a routine that gives all students the opportunity to briefly share ideas with a partner. Use this routine as an alternative to hand raising to allow all students to respond to an open-ended question or to "get their ideas out."

ROUTINE IN ACTION

1 Turn toward your partner.

- Ask an open-ended question. *Let's turn and talk to retell the end of the story in our own words.*
- Tell partners to face each other and look each other in the eye to show that they are interested in what their partner has to say.

2 One partner talks. One partner listens.

- Provide a model response, as needed, to help students begin to articulate their thinking. *You can start by saying: In the end, _____. Then finish the sentence to tell what happened.*
- Tell partners who will share first and who will listen first.

3 Switch!

- Let partners know to switch roles.
- Use a signal to regain students' attention, if needed.
- Briefly acknowledge ideas you heard from various partners.

THINK-PAIR SHARE

THINK-PAIR-SHARE engages students in a collaborative conversation in response to a question that students think about, share ideas with a partner, and then share with the whole group. Use this routine to ask open-ended questions that are personal or text-based.

ROUTINE IN ACTION

1 Think

- Pair students and assign numbers (1, 2).
- Ask an open-ended question. *Get ready to talk about this question with your partner: What is something you want to practice?*
- Allow students several seconds to formulate their responses.

2 Pair

- Tell students which partner will respond first and allow time to share.
- Listen to students' responses to their partners and ask a few students with strong responses to share with the whole group.

3 Share

- Ask students you identified to share first.
- Continue the sharing by asking for volunteers.

SOLO CHAIR

SOLO CHAIR is a special routine for presenting writing or other work to the class. Use this routine to share published writing, final projects, or reading responses.

ROUTINE IN ACTION

1 Present your work.

- Reserve a special chair for this purpose and involve students in decorating it.
- Select a few students who will present. Ensure that all students share over time.
- Provide a few sentence starters to focus students' presentations, such as *Today I will talk about . . .* or *A skill I applied to my reading was . . . .*
- Consider having presenters rehearse with partners beforehand.
- Tell students to speak clearly and loudly enough for everyone to hear.

2 Listen to your classmates.

- Review the expectations for active listening—remind students to focus their eyes and ears on the presenter and to listen respectfully.
- Allow the presenter to select one or two classmates to give feedback. Explain that feedback must be respectful and helpful. Provide a few sentence starters to focus the feedback, such as *I liked . . .* or *My favorite part was . . . .*
- Remind the presenter to listen actively and respectfully to the feedback.

Supporting Reading Independence

Give students the tools they need to become independent—and enthusiastic—readers.

Organizing Your Classroom's Reading Center

Guiding and encouraging students to choose books they'll enjoy reading—to themselves and to others—can help to lay the groundwork for a lifetime of reading enjoyment.

The Reading Center can be one of the most exciting places in a classroom—a treasure trove of books—from which students choose what looks appealing to them. Here students can find a sense of agency and community—*they* choose what to read and *they* work together to help grow the collection.

Use these tips for building a Reading Center that students will gravitate to daily:

- Organize the library by genre, topic, or author, rather than by reading level. Imagine the Reading Center with an appealing bookstore layout.

- Bring students together to help decide exactly how to organize the library. This fosters feelings of investment and community.

- You don't need to have your Reading Center perfectly assembled on the first day of school. In fact, it's better to have it unfinished so that students can contribute to its organization and structure over time. Start off with a small stack of engaging titles, including the *Into Reading* **Student Choice Library**. Survey students to find out what else they're interested in. Then, let the collection grow organically throughout the year, adding books from the school library, from donations, or from other sources. Continue to survey students periodically for their reading recommendations and try to add these to the Reading Center.

- Create a display with a few featured books and change them periodically to keep the Reading Center new and interesting throughout the year. You may want to put a different student or student pair in charge of the Reading Center display every two to four weeks. Give them ownership and watch their love of reading grow!

- As the library grows, make sure it reflects the diversity of the class. For more on this, see pages 56–57 for Creating a Culturally Responsive Environment.

GRADE 3
Student Choice Library

GRADE 4
Student Choice Library

GRADE 5
Student Choice Library

Self-Selecting Books

Once the classroom Reading Center is set up and ready to grow, it's time for students to start choosing what to read. Consider the following to support students' selection process:

- Model choosing a book. Pick one up and check out the cover. "This book is about planets. I love outer space! I'm going to read this." Or, "Cats are nice, but I'd rather read about something else right now. I'll put this book back and keep searching."

- Encourage students to examine a book's illustrations, photos, and graphics as another way to decide whether or not to choose it.

- Have students conduct short Book Talks to recommend to their classmates books they have read and enjoyed.

Setting Goals and Responding to Reading

When it comes to the amount of time students spend reading in one sitting, starting small is key. At the beginning of the year, that could look something like this:

- 10–15 minutes of reading

- a quick break to move and stretch

- another 10–15 minutes of reading

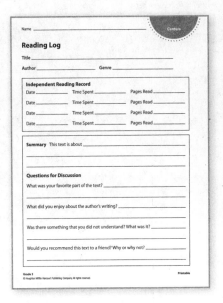

Of course, the more students read, the more they'll be *able to* read. Encourage them to set goals for how much time they will spend reading each day. Get them involved in tracking their progress by using the **Reading Log Printable**. As students head into independent reading time, have them set goals based on their reading history and how they're feeling in that moment.

Remember, while some students will find setting goals motivating, others may find it intimidating. Encourage students to see their reading time targets as how long they get to do something exciting and enjoyable!

Have students create a response journal in which they can document their responses to their independent reading books. Encourage students to note what they liked, what they didn't like, and why. Students may want to create a cover to personalize their journals. Review students' journals occasionally to note and discuss with them their reading preferences.

TEACHER → TEACHER
From the Classroom

❝ *You know how kids love to keep track of their height on the wall? Approach tracking reading the same way. Make it visual. You could do a colorful graph. Letting them literally see their progress is a game-changer.* ❞

¡Viva el español!

Bienvenidos a ¡Arriba la Lectura!

¡Arriba la Lectura! proporciona una amplia gama de recursos paralelos al programa *Into Reading* en inglés, potenciando así una experiencia educativa equitativa para todos los estudiantes. Además, estos recursos se ven enriquecidos por herramientas y componentes exclusivos del programa en español. En estas páginas, podrá obtener un panorama general de los recursos que distinguen a *¡Arriba la Lectura!*

Literatura hispana y universal

Desarrolle los conocimientos a través de colecciones temáticas de distintos géneros.

- *¡Arriba la Lectura!* ofrece una rica variedad de literatura hispana y universal para todos los gustos e intereses.

- La exposición a una amplia gama de literatura hispana y universal amplía los horizontes intelectuales y culturales de los estudiantes hacia una sociedad global.

- Alma Flor Ada y F. Isabel Campoy revisaron todos los poemas, selecciones y traducciones literarias para garantizar la excelencia en el uso del lenguaje y la literatura en español.

- Puede usar la **Revista Aventuras** para el tiempo de lectura y conversación en grupos pequeños.

- En **"Nuestra lengua es arte"**, encontrará experiencias culturales y lingüísticas relevantes.

Las **obras premiadas,** relevantes y culturalmente significativas, tanto de autores hispanos como de diversas partes del mundo, son una herramienta fundamental para enriquecer los conocimientos y destrezas de lectoescritura de todos los estudiantes, así como su herencia cultural.

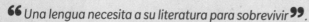

❝ *Una lengua necesita a su literatura para sobrevivir* **❞**.
— F. Isabel Campoy y Alma Flor Ada

Lecciones de destrezas fundamentales

¡Arriba la Lectura! desarrolla las destrezas de audición, expresión oral, lectura, escritura y reflexión que preparan a los estudiantes para una lectoescritura exitosa de por vida.

- Involucre activamente a los estudiantes en el **desarrollo de la conciencia fonológica** a través de una secuencia desarrollada especialmente para el español.

- Brinde una **enseñanza explícita de la fonética** para conectar la escritura con el habla, para leer y combinar sílabas y palabras.

- Enseñe a los estudiantes a leer y escribir **palabras de uso frecuente** específicas de la lengua española.

- Use **textos decodificables** para aplicar las destrezas aprendidas, practicar las palabras de uso frecuente en contexto y ayudar a los estudiantes a tener éxito en sus primeras experiencias de lectura independiente.

- Despierte el interés de los estudiantes por el **desarrollo de las destrezas fundamentales** con poemas originales en español.

Extensión lingüística

Apoye el lenguaje académico y promueva el aprecio de los estudiantes por la lengua y la cultura.

- Desarrolle la **conciencia metalingüística** con la sección **"Extensión lingüística"**.

- Comience a desarrollar la **alfabetización académica en español** con "Extensión lingüística".

Taller de escritura

- A medida que exploran y aplican el proceso de escritura, use las notas a la mano para brindar apoyo a los estudiantes de enseñanza dual.

- Observe que ciertos textos modelo están escritos originalmente en español.

Evaluación que toma en cuenta el lenguaje

- Estrategias, formularios y herramientas que ayudan a los maestros a interpretar e informar sobre los datos de una forma adecuada para los estudiantes de idiomas

- Consejos claros y útiles de parte de la Dra. Elena Izquierdo en el recurso **Lenguaje dual: Guía de implementación**

- Listas de comprobación observacionales, formularios de informe de lenguaje dual y pautas de calificación del desarrollo del lenguaje

- Herramientas simples para ayudar a los estudiantes a monitorear su propia biliteracidad

¡Viva el español!

Equidad y más

¡Arriba la Lectura! ofrece gran variedad de **literatura y materiales de enseñanza** especiales para el español, desarrollados y revisados por nuestras autoras.

Materiales para estudiantes

- Todas las selecciones de las **Lecturas en voz alta** y los **Superlibros** fueron revisadas por Alma Flor Ada y F. Isabel Campoy para asegurar la excelencia en el uso del lenguaje y la literatura en español.

- Los estudiantes podrán leer **poemas** divertidos y originales de Alma Flor Ada, F. Isabel Campoy y otros autores hispanohablantes para que las lecciones de destrezas fundamentales resulten entretenidas y apropiadas.

- Los **Alfamigos** incluyen canciones pegadizas que serán un éxito entre sus estudiantes. Tanto los **Videos** como las **Tarjetas de Alfamigos** brindan una amplia gama de posibilidades para la enseñanza de la lectoescritura.

- Los **Superlibros de rimas** fueron desarrollados por Alma Flor Ada y F. Isabel Campoy especialmente para *¡Arriba la Lectura!*

- La **Revista Aventuras** está compuesta por seis libros con literatura de calidad para enriquecer el desarrollo del lenguaje en español y la comprensión.

Materiales para maestros

- **"Nuestra lengua es arte",** un tesoro de la literatura en español creado por Alma Flor Ada y F. Isabel Campoy para la lectura en voz alta

- **"Extensión lingüística",** una sección pensada para enriquecer y ampliar la lectoescritura en español que contiene lecciones para la **Revista Aventuras** y "Nuestra lengua es arte"

- **Lecciones de destrezas fundamentales** especialmente diseñadas para el español

- **Notas especiales** para los contextos de enseñanza dual en cada lección

- **"Puente interlingüístico"** para desarrollar los conocimientos metalingüísticos en cada lección y conectar el aprendizaje en ambas lenguas

- El recurso **Lenguaje dual: Guía de implementación,** para facilitar el uso de *¡Arriba la Lectura!* e *Into Reading* en contextos de enseñanza dual

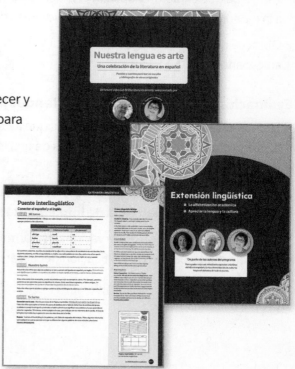

Destrezas fundamentales

Los materiales en los que se basa la enseñanza de las destrezas fundamentales
fueron creados específicamente para el aprendizaje del idioma español.

Lecturas iniciales

Aprende y demuestra

Tarjetas de fotos

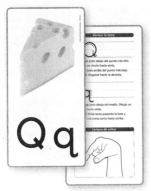

Tarjetas del abecedario

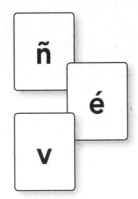

Tarjetas de letras

Tarjetas de Alfamigos

Tarjetas de palabras

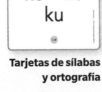

**Tarjetas de sílabas
y ortografía**

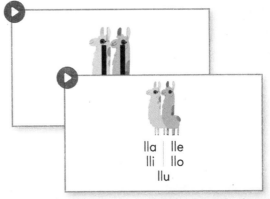

Videos de Alfamigos

Equidad y más *(cont.)*

Diseñado para la enseñanza bilingüe y de lenguaje dual

¡Arriba la Lectura! fue especialmente diseñado para su utilización en contextos de enseñanza dual, con secciones especiales que incluyen estrategias fáciles de usar y basadas en la investigación, tanto durante el tiempo de trabajo en grupos como durante el tiempo de trabajo de toda la clase.

- Los **materiales** han sido desarrollados con el asesoramiento de la Dra. Elena Izquierdo, profesional con vasta experiencia y especialidad en el desarrollo de programas bilingües y duales exitosos.

- El recurso de educación dual **Lenguaje dual: Guía de implementación,** desarrollado con el asesoramiento de la Dra. Izquierdo, ofrece guías de planificación sugerida, buenas prácticas y otros recursos útiles para potenciar el progreso de los maestros junto con sus estudiantes.

- La sección **"Análisis lingüístico contrastivo"** del recurso **Lenguaje dual: Guía de implementación** brinda información de fácil acceso y consejos de enseñanza para fomentar el desarrollo paralelo del español y el inglés.

- Las **estrategias** de **"Dual Language Settings"** ayudan a los maestros a implementar buenas prácticas justo donde y cuando las necesitan.

- Las notas en el punto de uso están destinadas a brindar apoyo a toda la diversidad de estudiantes.

- Cada lección incluye un **"Puente interlingüístico"** para ayudar a los estudiantes y maestros a desarrollar la comprensión metalingüística.

- Este programa brinda apoyo a los estudiantes, tanto en contextos de un idioma como en contextos de enseñanza dual.

- El programa está basado en un **modelo de enriquecimiento** y desarrollado en función de los conocimientos previos de los estudiantes.

- Los **videos de desarrollo profesional** ofrecen modelos de enseñanza de distintos aspectos del lenguaje dual que los maestros pueden aplicar en su propio salón de clases.

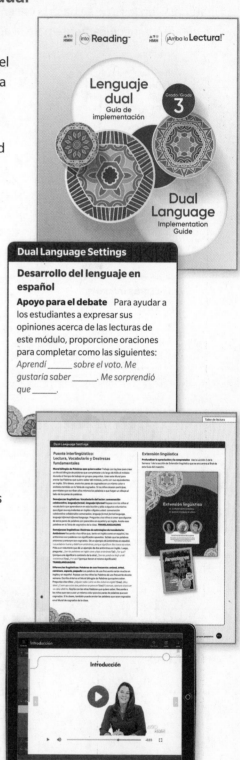

Nuestras autoras

El programa ¡*Arriba la Lectura!* fue creado en conjunto por el mismo grupo de autores que elaboró el programa *Into Reading*. Sin embargo, las autoras que aparecen en esta página estuvieron involucradas de forma particular en el desarrollo de ¡*Arriba la Lectura!* desde un principio para garantizar su calidad literaria, educativa y lingüística en el idioma español y para planificar las oportunidades de implementación junto con *Into Reading* para los contextos de enseñanza dual.

F. Isabel Campoy, M.A., Lic.

Autora bilingüe que ha recibido múltiples premios por sus más de 150 libros para niños, que incluyen poesía, teatro, cuentos, biografías, arte y cultura. Académica de reconocimiento internacional, docente y traductora. Miembro de la Academia Norteamericana de la Lengua Española.

Alma Flor Ada, Ph.D.

Profesora Emérita de la Universidad de San Francisco. Experta de renombre internacional en literatura y lectoescritura bilingües. Autora de más de 200 libros premiados, tanto académicos como para jóvenes lectores, y consejera líder en educación transformadora.

> **"Una lengua necesita a su literatura para sobrevivir"**.
> — F. Isabel Campoy y Alma Flor Ada

Elena Izquierdo, Ph.D.

Profesora asociada de formación docente en la Universidad de Texas, en El Paso. Investigadora y profesional cuyos focos son la enseñanza dual, la lectoescritura bilingüe y la equidad educativa para estudiantes de inglés.

> **"Los programas duales bien implementados ayudan a los niños a ser exitosos a través de ambos lenguajes y además, a desarrollar habilidades meta cognitivas y meta lingüísticas"**.
> — Dra. Elena Izquierdo

¡Viva el español!

Literatura hispana

¡Arriba la Lectura! contiene obras originales en español, seleccionadas por su calidad literaria y relevancia cultural. La exposición a una amplia gama de literatura escrita originalmente en español es fundamental para desarrollar la riqueza lingüística de los estudiantes y expandir sus horizontes intelectuales y culturales hacia una sociedad global.

Lecturas para desarrollar la comprensión

Las lecturas de *mi*Libro, los **Superlibros**, los **Libros para la lectura en voz alta,** los **Textos de enfoque** y las **Lecturas iniciales** presentan contenidos multiculturales que despiertan el interés de los estudiantes y son una herramienta imprescindible para enriquecer los conocimientos y desarrollar la comprensión.

Se han desarrollado especialmente para el programa textos de diversos géneros, como el *Superlibro de rimas* y la selección *El alegre abecedario,* y muchos otros títulos de F. Isabel Campoy y Alma Flor Ada, además de las **Lecturas iniciales,** escritas en su mayoría por autores hispanos específicamente para este programa.

Lecturas para desarrollar las destrezas fundamentales

Las **Lecturas iniciales** fueron cuidadosamente desarrolladas para este programa. Estos textos decodificables contienen exclusivamente los elementos de fonética, las sílabas y las palabras de uso frecuente que han sido enseñados previamente e incluyen un tema o un argumento presente en todos los textos de la semana para desarrollar la expectativa y despertar el interés de los estudiantes. Su principal objetivo es afianzar la comprensión lectora, dado que en español la decodificación no representa un reto significativo.

> ❝ *Debido a que el español tiene una relación más consistente con el sonido de las letras, los problemas de decodificación no son tan frecuentes como los problemas de comprensión* ❞.

— Dra. Elena Izquierdo

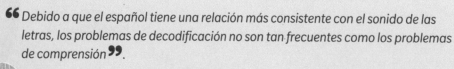
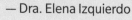

Poesía

¡Arriba la Lectura! incluye poesía escrita originalmente en español, la cual resulta esencial para el desarrollo de las destrezas fundamentales, el enriquecimiento del lenguaje y la comprensión.

Se puede hallar poesía escrita originalmente en español como práctica oral en las lecciones de fonética de la **Guía del maestro** y en las páginas de **Mostrar y motivar** de los Grados K–2. También se encuentran poemas originales en español en las **Ediciones del estudiante** y en los **Textos de enfoque** de los Grados 3–6.

Selecciones multimedia

Videos de cierre y de selección

Los videos creados exclusivamente para *¡Arriba la Lectura!* proporcionan un modo diferente y entretenido de presentar contenidos para que los estudiantes comenten y desarrollen las habilidades para participar en conversaciones.

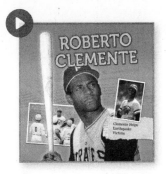

Videos de Alfamigos

Los **Videos de Alfamigos** fueron creados especialmente para este programa por músicos profesionales, utilizando diferentes ritmos musicales y canciones pegadizas. Su propósito es enseñar a los estudiantes las letras, los dígrafos y las sílabas de una forma atractiva.

Los **Alfamigos** son amenos y divertidos, por lo que llaman la atención de los estudiantes al tiempo que fortalecen sus destrezas de lectoescritura y los ayudan a decodificar las sílabas que están aprendiendo.

¡Más literatura hispana!

Revista Aventuras

Los textos de la **Revista Aventuras,** escritos originalmente en español, cuentan con bellas ilustraciones y se pueden usar para enriquecer el lenguaje académico, la comprensión y la apreciación literaria. Estas lecturas incluyen cuentos, textos informativos, biografías, artículos, novelas históricas, poemas, etc. Su propósito es inspirar a los estudiantes y despertar en ellos el placer de la lectura.

Nuestra lengua es arte

Esta sección presenta literatura original en español de gran relevancia cultural, seleccionada por las autoras Alma Flor Ada y F. Isabel Campoy, para que el maestro comparta con la clase en voz alta al finalizar cada módulo de la **Guía del maestro** de los Grados K–6.

En "Nuestra lengua es arte", los estudiantes encontrarán experiencias culturales y lingüísticas relevantes, ya que la celebración de las diversas culturas del mundo está muy presente en los temas abordados. Incluye una sección de libros recomendados de autores de diversos orígenes hispanos para que los estudiantes exploren nuevas lecturas.

Superlibros de apoyo

Los **Superlibros de rimas** de los Grados K-1 y *El ABC de Culebra* fueron creados especialmente en español para *¡Arriba la Lectura!* Las rimas ayudan a desarrollar las destrezas fundamentales y permiten a los estudiantes compartir lecturas y mejorar la comprensión auditiva, mientras que *El ABC de Culebra* ofrece un repaso de las letras del abecedario acompañadas de bellas imágenes que les permiten establecer asociaciones útiles.

Interacción con *Into Reading*

Temas culturalmente relevantes

Los estudiantes tienen acceso a lecturas en inglés sobre temas relevantes relacionados con la cultura hispanoamericana, como "Pepita and the Bully", *Mango, Abuela, and me* y "Safeguarding the California Coast".

Paridad temática

Los temas cubiertos mediante la literatura original en español y en inglés se corresponden entre sí, lo cual potencia la implementación de programas de educación de lenguaje dual. Asimismo, los apartados de lenguaje dual brindan consejos de enseñanza para fomentar el desarrollo paralelo del español y el inglés y permiten comparar y contrastar ambos idiomas.

Versiones en español de excelencia

Todas las lecturas han sido cuidadosamente revisadas por Alma Flor Ada y F. Isabel Campoy para asegurar la excelencia en el uso del lenguaje y la literatura en español y para garantizar que las traducciones literarias son de gran calidad, escritas con un lenguaje auténtico y natural.

Literatura universal

Asegurar la diversidad cultural de la literatura que leen los estudiantes es de suma importancia. Por ello, *¡Arriba la Lectura!* incluye lecturas escritas por autores de los más diversos países y culturas y los temas tratados responden a esa diversidad.

La multiculturalidad de los autores hispanos se ve reflejada en sus variados orígenes, con autores de Argentina, México, Chile, El Salvador, Nicaragua, Puerto Rico, España, Estados Unidos y Cuba, entre muchos otros. Esta diversidad proporciona una mayor riqueza al lenguaje aprendido por los estudiantes y una visión del mundo más amplia y libre de prejuicios.

Lecturas bilingües

Las lecturas bilingües son de gran importancia para el desarrollo de las destrezas lingüísticas de los estudiantes tanto en inglés como en español, ya que les permiten establecer conexiones entre ambos idiomas y apoyarse en el dominio de la lengua nativa para fortalecer las destrezas de lectoescritura en la lengua que aprenden.

Enseñanza especializada

Currículo especializado para el español

Para desarrollar una buena alfabetización en español, la educación debe basarse en las características específicas de la lengua española. La enseñanza de la lectura y escritura en español no puede ser una réplica o una traducción directa de la enseñanza en inglés.

¡Arriba la Lectura! está especialmente diseñado para abordar las particularidades de la lengua española y cumplir con los estándares de enseñanza. Este diseño educativo comienza con las destrezas fundamentales de lectura y escritura.

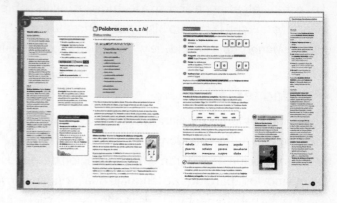

Aprendizaje inicial de los sonidos de las letras

En español, es fundamental aprender primero los sonidos de las letras, en lugar de los nombres de las letras. Como los sonidos de las vocales en español son los mismos que los nombres de las vocales, y los nombres de las consonantes incluyen sonidos de vocal que pueden contaminar la correspondencia entre letras y sonidos, la enseñanza de los nombres de las letras debe posponerse hasta que los lectores dominen las relaciones grafema-fonema.

¡Arriba la Lectura! presenta los nombres de las letras gradualmente mediante una rutina de conocimiento de las letras cada dos semanas para exponer a los estudiantes a la noción del abecedario. Los nombres de las letras y el abecedario se refuerzan aún más durante la semana dedicada al abecedario.

Para el Grado 1, se entiende que los estudiantes tienen el suficiente conocimiento previo de los nombres de las letras en español y los sonidos aprendidos durante el kínder para continuar reforzándolos semanalmente.

El español es una lengua basada en sílabas

Una vez que los estudiantes han aprendido las vocales y sus sonidos correspondientes, aprenden a formar sílabas. *¡Arriba la Lectura!* combina el método silábico, que se enfoca en la unidad más amplia de la sílaba, con el

> 66 *Enseñar los fonemas de las consonantes individuales tiene sentido en inglés, pero en el español hablado, los fonemas de consonantes nunca se pronuncian sin vocales, por lo que enseñar consonantes de forma aislada suena artificial y es ajeno a nuestro idioma* 99 .
>
> — Alma Flor Ada

método global, que presenta contextos significativos a través de palabras, frases, rimas u oraciones para luego enfocarse en sus elementos: sílabas, sonidos y letras.

La ortografía transparente del español

La lengua española tiene una ortografía transparente. Cada una de las cinco vocales tiene siempre el mismo sonido y la mayoría de las consonantes representan un solo sonido. Debido a esto, la adquisición de destrezas de decodificación ocurre más rápidamente en español que en inglés.

Debido a la ortografía transparente del idioma español, los estudiantes que trabajan con *¡Arriba la Lectura!* comienzan a dominar la decodificación en el kínder y pueden aprender eficazmente todas las sílabas y los patrones de ortografía de los sonidos para el final del Grado 1. En el Grado 2, la enseñanza se centra en dominar los patrones dentro de las palabras polisílabas y enfocarse en la comprensión en español durante todo el proceso de lectura.

Palabras de uso frecuente en español

La ortografía transparente de la lengua española produce patrones fácilmente decodificables, de modo que la lectura no requiere de tanta práctica en la construcción de la memoria visual para las palabras vistas. Las palabras de uso frecuente en *¡Arriba la Lectura!* han sido seleccionadas en base a listas de palabras de uso frecuente en español y a una sección transversal de listas investigadas específicamente para el aprendizaje de las artes del lenguaje en español. Aprender a reconocer fácilmente estas palabras promueve la fluidez.

Literatura escrita originalmente en español

Los cuentos, las selecciones de no ficción y los poemas originales con gran riqueza de vocabulario de *¡Arriba la Lectura!* constituyen una parte crucial de la educación especializada para el español. A medida que los estudiantes entran en contacto con esta literatura escrita y cuidadosamente seleccionada para representar la variedad y riqueza del idioma español, amplían la comprensión, el repertorio de vocabulario, las expresiones idiomáticas y los modismos en español.

Ortografía y gramática específicas del español

La **Guía del maestro** de *¡Arriba la Lectura!* aborda temas de ortografía y gramática que son específicos del idioma español, entre ellos el uso de mayúsculas, la puntuación en los diálogos y la concordancia de pronombre-sujeto. Dentro del **"Taller de escritura",** *¡Arriba la Lectura!* ofrece enseñanza adicional sobre la ortografía y gramática específicas del idioma español en el contexto de la escritura, que incluye acentuación, conjugaciones de verbos, concordancia de género y sujeto tácito.

La ortografía transparente es una correspondencia prácticamente perfecta entre las letras y los sonidos en un idioma. Hace que sea fácil para el lector saber cómo se pronuncia una palabra escrita.

Las palabras polisílabas (de varias sílabas) son comunes en español, pero son fácilmente decodificables para los estudiantes.

Pedagogía intercultural

El programa *¡Arriba la Lectura!* se fundamenta en la pedagogía intercultural como modo de integrar a todos los estudiantes de cada salón de clases, sea cual fuere el entorno cultural del que procedan.

¿Qué es la pedagogía intercultural?

La pedagogía intercultural está diseñada intencionalmente para acoger el trasfondo cultural de todos los estudiantes. Se basa en la profunda comprensión del papel fundamental que desempeña la cultura en el proceso de aprendizaje. Todos los componentes de *¡Arriba la Lectura!* están diseñados especialmente para plasmar la interculturalidad de los salones de clases.

La pedagogía intercultural comienza cuando vemos como ventajas las diferencias que nuestros estudiantes aportan a los salones de clases. Para los estudiantes bilingües emergentes, esto significa que consideramos su idioma principal como un atributo. Buscamos siempre oportunidades para incrementar las destrezas y el conocimiento que nuestros estudiantes han desarrollado en su idioma primario y diseñamos un currículo que los ayude a reconocer estos atributos y a progresar a partir de ellos. Motivamos el uso del repertorio completo que cada estudiante tiene en ambos idiomas con el propósito de que puedan comunicarse, aprender y expresar su identidad al máximo.

El maestro actúa principalmente como facilitador del aprendizaje, seleccionando oportunidades enriquecedoras para que los estudiantes colaboren y participen en conversaciones con sus compañeros.

¡Arriba la Lectura! sugiere actividades de aprendizaje que ayudan a los maestros a conocer a cada uno de sus estudiantes como individuo (sus puntos fuertes, sus dificultades, sus intereses y su trasfondo familiar y cultural) a través de proyectos y propuestas de escritura. A lo largo del programa, los estudiantes pueden elegir entre actividades, textos y proyectos, lo que les permite explorar sus intereses individuales y aprender dentro del contexto de su cultura y sus experiencias previas.

Las actividades de *¡Arriba la Lectura!* están diseñadas para brindar a los estudiantes oportunidades para conectar su aprendizaje con su propio trasfondo a través de distintas secciones que los ayudan a relacionar el texto que leen con la comunidad, con sus propias experiencias y con su cultura.

Una clase con sensibilidad intercultural se focaliza en los estudiantes.

Los esfuerzos por incluir a la familia van mucho más allá de la tradicional reunión de padres y maestros, en la cual el papel del maestro es compartir información con los padres sobre el desempeño del estudiante en la escuela. En las escuelas con sensibilidad intercultural, los maestros buscan aprender activamente sobre la familia de cada estudiante y sus tradiciones, creencias y perspectivas en torno a la educación y el aprendizaje. Se comprometen con las familias como miembros del mismo equipo para apoyar el desarrollo académico y socioemocional del estudiante.

¡Arriba la Lectura! incluye varios recursos para ayudar a los maestros a involucrar a las familias, como parte del equipo, en el proceso educativo. Estos recursos incluyen las **"Cartas para la familia"** y las **Páginas imprimibles** de la sección **"Relacionarse con las familias"** que los estudiantes pueden llevarse a casa. Las "Cartas para la familia" recomiendan lecturas adicionales escritas originalmente en español.

La cuidadosa y atenta selección de los materiales de enseñanza es un componente esencial de una clase con sensibilidad intercultural. Es crucial que los estudiantes se vean a sí mismos reflejados en los libros que leen. Los estudiantes se benefician de la lectura habitual de textos que incluyan sucesos con los que se puedan identificar y personajes que compartan sus trasfondos culturales y hablen su mismo idioma. Lo ideal es que los materiales de enseñanza incluyan selecciones escritas por autores diversos, incluidos aquellos que compartan los trasfondos lingüísticos y culturales de los estudiantes de la clase.

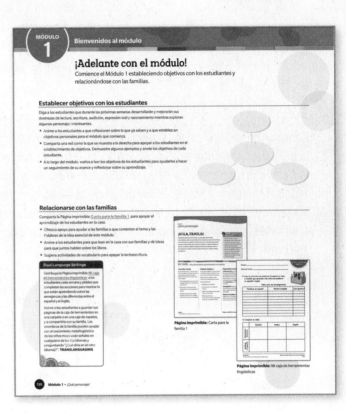

En los entornos de lenguaje dual, esto significa que los materiales en español deben incluir una abundancia de textos escritos originalmente en español por autores que representen la diversidad de la comunidad hispana. Tanto los materiales como la enseñanza con sensibilidad intercultural desafían los estereotipos predominantes y fomentan perspectivas positivas.

¡Arriba la Lectura! celebra la riqueza de la literatura hispana. Los textos de autores hispanos representan casi el 60% de los textos en todos los niveles de grado, entre ellos canciones y cuentos tradicionales, así como textos de autores reconocidos como Graciela Montes, José Martí, Amado Nervo, Suni Paz, Rubén Darío, Georgina Lázaro, María Elena Walsh y Jorge Urgueta.

Los autores de *¡Arriba la Lectura!* provienen de una variedad de países de habla hispana, entre ellos Argentina, España, Cuba, México, Puerto Rico, Nicaragua,

Pedagogía intercultural *(cont.)*

Chile, Colombia, Ecuador y El Salvador. La **Revista Aventuras** y la sección "Nuestra lengua es arte" contienen literatura escrita en español que expone a los estudiantes a la riqueza y diversidad de vocabulario y contenidos que representan al mundo de habla hispana.

Además de la amplia gama de textos que representan a las culturas hispanas, *¡Arriba la Lectura!* también incluye una variedad de textos que representan la diversidad de nuestras escuelas y nuestra nación. Así, los estudiantes se ven reflejados en los textos que leen y quedan expuestos, además, a una variedad de culturas diferentes.

> ❝*Tanto en casa como en la escuela, los libros se eligen con cuidado: libros que representan los valores de la cultura, la riqueza del patrimonio, la universalidad de la experiencia humana. Esos libros pueden contribuir a enriquecer las identidades de los niños. A través de ellos, los niños aprenden a explorar quiénes son y a comprender el mundo en el que viven. En esas páginas, ven similitudes y diferencias entre sus comunidades, tradiciones y visiones del mundo. Y pueden aprender sobre la igualdad, la justicia, la libertad y el amor* ❞.
>
> — F. Isabel Campoy

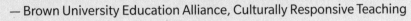

> *Una pedagogía que reconoce, responde y celebra culturas fundamentales ofrece un acceso pleno y equitativo a la educación para estudiantes de todas las culturas*.
> — Brown University Education Alliance, *Culturally Responsive Teaching*

¿Por qué planificar una pedagogía intercultural?

Cuando la enseñanza y los materiales responden principalmente a la cultura dominante de Estados Unidos y esperan que los estudiantes vean la escuela y el aprendizaje desde esa perspectiva, se les niega a los estudiantes de diversos orígenes el mismo acceso a todo lo que la escuela tiene para ofrecer.

Al diseñar intencionalmente escuelas y salones de clases que reciban con los brazos abiertos a todas las culturas de nuestra comunidad, creamos las condiciones para que todos los estudiantes tengan las mismas oportunidades para aprender y prosperar.

La educación con sensibilidad intercultural es el vehículo a través del cual logramos la equidad.

Las investigaciones demuestran el impacto positivo de la enseñanza con sensibilidad intercultural en la motivación y el compromiso de los estudiantes.

Cuando los estudiantes pueden conectar su aprendizaje en clase con sus experiencias personales fuera de la escuela, el aprendizaje se vuelve relevante y ameno.

> *Las investigaciones han demostrado que ninguna estrategia de enseñanza involucrará sistemáticamente a todos los estudiantes. La clave es ayudar a los estudiantes a relacionar el contenido de las lecciones con sus propios orígenes*.
> — Wlodkowski, R. & Ginsberg, M. (1995). A Framework for Culturally Responsive Teaching. *Educational Leadership, 53*(1), 17–21.

La participación y la motivación de los estudiantes son factores críticos en la persistencia y el éxito escolar a largo plazo. Al diseñar intencionalmente una enseñanza con sensibilidad intercultural, comenzando en los primeros grados, creamos las condiciones para que los estudiantes sientan una firme conexión con la escuela y sigan participando en el aprendizaje a lo largo de su experiencia escolar.

Puentes interlingüísticos

Cuando a los estudiantes se les brinda la oportunidad de utilizar toda la gama de recursos lingüísticos que poseen, aprenden de manera significativa y aprovechan al máximo su potencial.

Todos los estudiantes bilingües emergentes llegan a la escuela con la capacidad de usar lo que saben sobre el lenguaje para apoyar el proceso que los convertirá en completamente bilingües. De hecho, cada estudiante posee un conjunto particular de recursos lingüísticos que no se limitan a un idioma u otro. Cuando consiguen hacer conexiones entre idiomas, los estudiantes pueden usar los recursos lingüísticos que ya tienen para ampliar el aprendizaje en ambos idiomas.

> ❝ *Cuando los estudiantes pueden reflexionar sobre todas sus prácticas lingüísticas es cuando se desarrolla el lenguaje* ❞.
>
> — Joanna Yip y Ofelia García

Sin embargo, no podemos esperar que los estudiantes reconozcan automáticamente las conexiones entre los idiomas. Una estrategia importante basada en la investigación es el puente interlingüístico. El puente es un paso crucial en el desarrollo de la alfabetización bilingüe de los estudiantes.

Los "Puentes interlingüísticos" de *¡Arriba la Lectura!*

Cada lección de *¡Arriba la Lectura!* cuenta con páginas dedicadas al "Puente interlingüístico", sección que brinda oportunidades de enriquecimiento del idioma basadas en el contenido de la lección específica trabajada. Estos puentes interlingüísticos resaltan las similitudes y diferencias entre los temas concretos del inglés y del español cubiertos en esa lección. Sirven como una base que los maestros pueden utilizar para incorporar más oportunidades de realizar conexiones en sus grupos.

El puente interlingüístico alude a la práctica de poner ambos idiomas uno junto al otro e identificar y enseñar explícitamente los puntos en común y las diferencias que existen entre ellos.

El translenguaje es el uso fluido de todos los recursos lingüísticos presentes en el repertorio de un estudiante para comunicarse y aprender, independientemente del idioma utilizado.

> ❝ *La enseñanza basada en el translenguaje también debe desarrollarse. Esto incluye tener el material multilingüe apropiado para que los estudiantes aprendan en ambos idiomas, preparar el salón de clases como un espacio multilingüe y agrupar a los estudiantes según el idioma que hablan en casa para que puedan ayudarse mutuamente y profundizar el significado del aprendizaje. E implica, también, diseñar intencionalmente lecciones con un lenguaje, un contenido y unos objetivos específicos. Una lección y un diseño de unidad de translenguaje no pueden generarse por casualidad, sino que deben integrarse plenamente en la lección* ❞.
>
> — Joanna Yip y Ofelia García

A los estudiantes se les presentan las similitudes y diferencias entre el inglés y el español relacionadas con un tema de la lección.

Los estudiantes reconocen e identifican las similitudes y las diferencias entre el inglés y el español, guiados por el maestro.

Los estudiantes tienen la posibilidad de participar según el nivel de adquisición del lenguaje que posean.

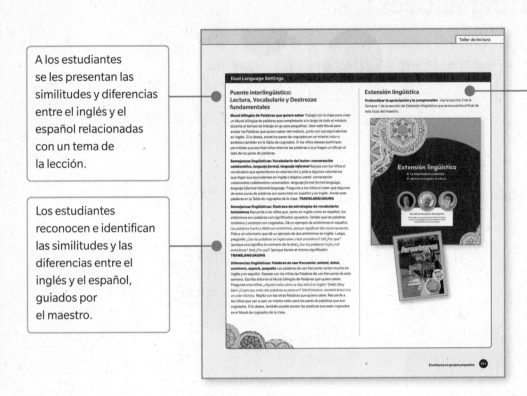

Los objetivos del "Puente interlingüístico" son:

- Creación de conexiones entre el contenido aprendido en un idioma y ese mismo contenido en otro idioma
- Desarrollo del vocabulario académico relacionado con el tema trabajado en la lección, en inglés y en español*
- Participación en el análisis lingüístico contrastivo
- Desarrollo de la conciencia metalingüística

*El recurso **Lenguaje dual: Guía de implementación** proporciona actividades adicionales relacionadas con cada módulo encaminadas a ampliar el vocabulario académico interdisciplinario de los estudiantes tanto en inglés como en español.

Es importante tener en cuenta que existe una transferencia tanto positiva como negativa entre los idiomas. Ambos son igualmente importantes para enseñar a los estudiantes bilingües.

La transferencia positiva ocurre cuando el conocimiento de un idioma facilita el aprendizaje en otro idioma.

La transferencia negativa ocurre cuando el conocimiento de un idioma interfiere o causa errores en el aprendizaje de un nuevo idioma.

El lenguaje no se transfiere. Los conceptos de lenguaje, sí ".
— Dra. Elena Izquierdo

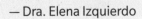

Puentes interlingüísticos (cont.)

En *¡Arriba la Lectura!*, los temas de transferencia positiva y negativa se presentan a los estudiantes en la sección "Puente interlingüístico" a través de las siguientes herramientas:

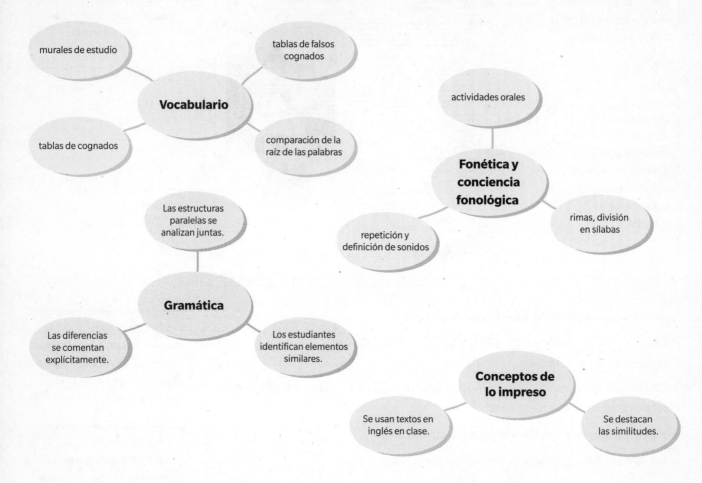

Para temas que son específicos del idioma español o que podrían crear una transferencia negativa, se ofrecen actividades de apoyo adicionales en español, como trabalenguas y dictados.

🔵 *Consulte la sección "Análisis lingüístico contrastivo" en las páginas E29–E40 de esta guía para obtener información más detallada sobre el análisis lingüístico contrastivo, el translenguaje y la conciencia metalingüística, así como temas específicos y sugerencias de actividades sobre la transferencia positiva y negativa entre el inglés y el español que se podrían tratar en clase.*

Extensión lingüística

La sección "Extensión lingüística" de *¡Arriba la Lectura!* proporciona textos culturalmente relevantes de literatura original en español para ampliar las destrezas de lenguaje y profundizar en la apreciación de las culturas hispanohablantes de todo el mundo.

Los textos de la **Revista Aventuras** fueron seleccionados por **Alma Flor Ada** y **F. Isabel Campoy,** académicas de reconocimiento internacional y autoras de cientos de libros premiados. Ambas autoras escribieron, además, los cuentos y poemas de la subsección **"Apreciar la lengua y la cultura".**

La **Dra. Elena Izquierdo,** investigadora especializada en la enseñanza dual y la lectoescritura bilingüe, ha supervisado de cerca **"La alfabetización académica",** subsección que incluye el **"Puente interlingüístico".**

La alfabetización académica

"La alfabetización académica" trabaja una selección de textos de la **Revista Aventuras,** la cual contiene decenas de textos escritos originalmente en español, ideales para desarrollar el lenguaje académico, la comprensión y la apreciación literaria. Las lecturas fueron especialmente seleccionadas con el objetivo de celebrar las culturas hispanas y teniendo en cuenta la riqueza lingüística y la calidad literaria de las obras. Los temas están relacionados con el tema del módulo, de manera que los estudiantes puedan establecer conexiones.

El apartado **"Vistazo rápido"** ofrece un panorama general sobre el texto principal y la lectura conjunta. Los textos se encuentran en la **Revista Aventuras,** acompañados de vistosas ilustraciones.

Se explican las razones por las cuales los textos han sido seleccionados y se presenta una breve biografía de los autores.

Se incluye una nota cultural que permite a los estudiantes establecer conexiones entre la lectura y la sociedad.

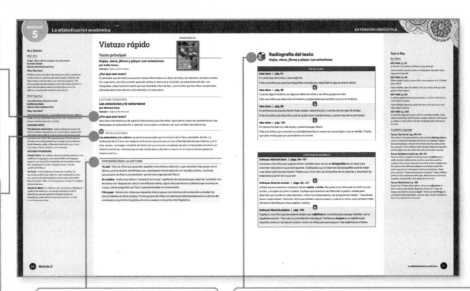

Se dan opciones para la lectura diferenciada según el nivel de aprendizaje de los estudiantes.

En **"Radiografía del texto",** se resumen las ideas clave de cada página y se ofrece una actividad para desarrollar el lenguaje académico.

¡VIVA EL ESPAÑOL!

Extensión lingüística (cont.)

El apartado **"Leamos juntos"** refuerza las estrategias de aprendizaje de palabras en el contexto de la lectura. Este apartado está diseñado para asistir al maestro mientras guía la lectura del texto principal.

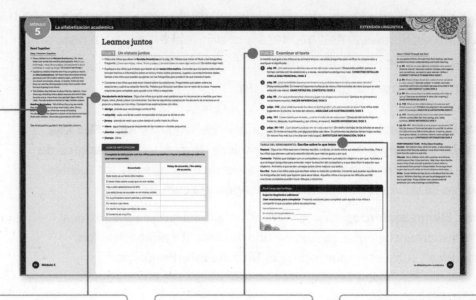

Se analizan palabras de vocabulario que pueden resultar desconocidas para los estudiantes.

Las preguntas de seguimiento ayudan a evaluar la comprensión y a desarrollar una lectura analítica.

Al final de este apartado, los estudiantes comparten sus ideas en conversaciones con un compañero y escriben sobre la lectura.

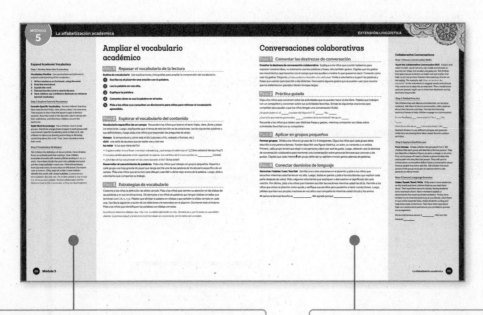

El apartado **"Ampliar el vocabulario académico"** se enfoca en el trabajo con el vocabulario nuevo y ayuda a los maestros a establecer estrategias para explorar las palabras que resultan desconocidas para los estudiantes mediante preguntas y explicaciones basadas en el contexto en el que aparecen las palabras.

Las **"Conversaciones colaborativas"** permiten desarrollar las destrezas de conversación de los estudiantes, profundizar en el pensamiento crítico y la conciencia metalingüística y aplicar el vocabulario aprendido. Este apartado también tiene como propósito conectar los diferentes dominios del lenguaje mediante la escritura de textos breves como respuesta a la lectura.

En el apartado **"Leer la lectura conjunta"**, el maestro lee en voz alta la lectura y hace preguntas para verificar la comprensión. Después de leer el texto varias veces, toda la clase analiza el significado y se establecen conexiones con otros textos.

El apartado **"Puente interlingüístico"** proporciona estrategias sencillas que permiten implementar prácticas para el desarrollo de las habilidades cognitivas en inglés y en español, evaluar el aprendizaje de los estudiantes y establecer conexiones entre ambos idiomas para profundizar la comprensión.

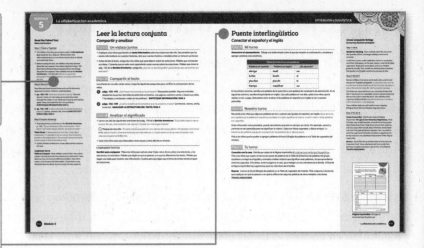

Apreciar la lengua y la cultura

La subsección "Apreciar la lengua y la cultura" presenta una selección de textos de "Nuestra lengua es arte": poemas y cuentos escritos originalmente en español por Alma Flor Ada y F. Isabel Campoy especialmente para este programa. Estos textos fueron seleccionados con el fin de que el maestro los comparta con la clase al finalizar cada módulo de la **Guía del maestro** y permitirán ampliar el vocabulario de los estudiantes y desarrollar su apreciación literaria.

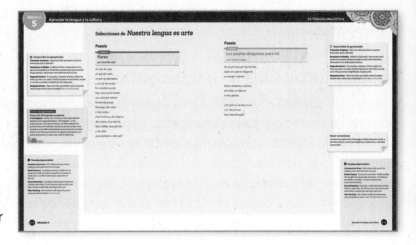

Los poemas y cuentos de "Nuestra lengua es arte" celebran la diversidad cultural. Esto queda demostrado por las constantes referencias a las culturas de todo el mundo y muy especialmente a las culturas hispanas. Esta sección incluye actividades para evaluar la comprensión, hacer conexiones con otras lecturas y desarrollar la apreciación literaria.

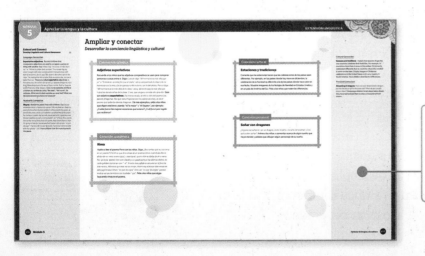

En el apartado **"Ampliar y conectar"**, se establecen conexiones lingüísticas, académicas, culturales y personales.

Lenguaje dual y biliteracidad

Un programa para la enseñanza en lenguaje dual

¡Arriba la Lectura! se creó intencionalmente para su uso conjunto con *Into Reading* en entornos de educación en lenguaje dual. Los temas se diseñaron para cubrir los estándares de enseñanza y se desarrollan de forma paralela en ambos programas, de modo que permiten ampliar los conocimientos de los estudiantes en los dos idiomas, según sus necesidades.

La temática de los módulos de *¡Arriba la Lectura!* e *Into Reading* se corresponde entre ambos programas para facilitar a los maestros la enseñanza en ambos idiomas según los objetivos de su programa.

Las secciones "Puente interlingüístico" y "Dual Language Settings" permiten establecer conexiones entre el español y el inglés en todas las lecciones de *¡Arriba la Lectura!* y fomentan un aprendizaje bilingüe que integra el desarrollo cognitivo de los estudiantes en ambos idiomas. Estas secciones se ven complementadas por el recurso **Lenguaje dual: Guía de implementación,** creado específicamente para este programa.

Lenguaje dual: Guía de implementación

Esta guía fue diseñada por la Dra. Elena Izquierdo, autora de *¡Arriba la Lectura!* y experta en educación dual y biliteracidad. Su propósito es orientar a los maestros en la enseñanza e implementación de programas de lenguaje dual y biliteracidad, de modo que puedan integrar de manera práctica y eficaz materiales de *¡Arriba la Lectura!* e *Into Reading* de una forma flexible, según sus propios objetivos. La guía consta de tres partes y pretende ser un recurso de fácil acceso para la consulta permanente, con un atractivo diseño que facilita la lectura y la navegación.

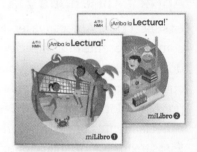

Parte 1: La adquisición del lenguaje en contextos bilingües

Esta sección presenta conceptos fundamentales de la biliteracidad (los diversos modelos de educación bilingüe, sus principios comunes, el desarrollo de la conciencia cultural, el translenguaje) y brinda un marco teórico desde el cual los maestros puedan abordar la enseñanza dual y comprender su relevancia. También incluye un glosario bilingüe de términos profesionales relacionados con la enseñanza dual y una bibliografía de investigaciones sobre la enseñanza del lenguaje en contextos bilingües.

Parte 2: Planificar para el grado

Esta sección práctica proporciona recursos para planificar las lecciones. **"Vocabulario intercurricular"** es un apartado de ampliación léxica y ofrece un selecto vocabulario cotidiano y académico en ambos idiomas relacionado con los temas que estudiarán los estudiantes a lo largo del grado.

Las listas de vocabulario intercurricular van acompañadas de definiciones, ejemplos de uso y actividades sugeridas con objeto de ampliar el vocabulario, desarrollar más los conocimientos de cada módulo y extenderlos a otras materias. Los temas de este apartado se corresponden con los estándares de enseñanza.

Por otra parte, **"Vistazo a la semana"** permite visualizar rápidamente los contenidos de cada semana para que el maestro elija qué temas cubrir en cada idioma y cómo conectarlos en su clase de enseñanza dual o biliteracidad.

Parte 3: Recursos

La tercera parte de la guía contiene fichas de registro de la evaluación dual, fichas para la planificación curricular, pautas de calificación y rutinas integradas para la biliteracidad. Incluye una rutina de dictado, con la que los estudiantes aplican los contenidos de artes del lenguaje que aprendieron con un ejercicio controlado, reflexionan sobre esos contenidos para desarrollar su conciencia metalingüística y los comparan y contrastan en ambos idiomas. Esta sección ayudará a los maestros con la implementación del programa de lenguaje dual de su preferencia.

> **"** *Para los niños que trabajan a través de dos idiomas, las evaluaciones en los dos idiomas son parte de una evaluación completa para poder hacer decisiones instruccionales* **"**.
>
> — Dra. Elena Izquierdo

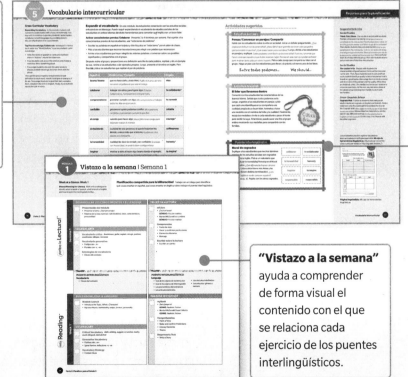

"Vocabulario intercurricular" contiene listas de vocabulario académico con definiciones, ejemplos de uso y actividades sugeridas.

"Puente interlingüístico" invita a trabajar con un mural de cognados para que los estudiantes establezcan conexiones entre ambos idiomas.

"Vistazo a la semana" ayuda a comprender de forma visual el contenido con el que se relaciona cada ejercicio de los puentes interlingüísticos.

Glosario de términos profesionales

Nota: Las definiciones reflejan usos comunes actuales. Existen diferencias significativas en el uso de los términos por parte de distintos educadores, principalmente porque el bilingüismo, la biliteracidad y los programas de lenguaje dual son campos de estudio que todavía se encuentran en desarrollo y expansión. El propósito de este glosario es contribuir a la estandarización de una terminología básica compartida.

A

adquisición del lenguaje (*language acquisition*) Trayectoria del desarrollo del lenguaje en los estudiantes que adquieren una primera y una segunda lengua; incluye lenguaje tanto receptivo como expresivo.

análisis lingüístico contrastivo (*contrastive analysis*) Práctica pedagógica en la que los estudiantes comparan y contrastan la morfología, la fonología, la sintaxis, la gramática o la pragmática de la lengua mayoritaria y de la lengua asociada.

B

bilingüismo (*bilingualism*) Capacidad de una persona para comunicarse en dos idiomas; el nivel de dominio de las destrezas para escuchar, hablar, leer y escribir en cada idioma puede ser muy variable en cada individuo y puede abarcar un amplio rango, desde un dominio básico del segundo idioma hasta el dominio total de ambos idiomas.

biliteracidad (*biliteracy*) Desarrollo de la lectoescritura en dos idiomas, que incluye todas las competencias lingüísticas, es decir, la comprensión auditiva, la lectura, la escritura y la expresión oral; también se conoce como "alfabetización bilingüe" y "lectoescritura bilingüe".

C

capacidad oral (*oracy*) Todas las destrezas de expresión oral y comprensión auditiva que se usan en el lenguaje oral. La capacidad oral es una de las bases fundamentales de la lectoescritura.

cartel didáctico (*anchor chart*) Representación visual de conceptos o del contenido de una lección expresados con dibujos y/o un lenguaje sencillo, a menudo creado por el maestro en colaboración con los estudiantes.

cognados (*cognates*) Palabras que suenan y se escriben de forma similar en dos idiomas y tienen la misma raíz.

conciencia metalingüística (*metalinguistic awareness*) Comprensión de cómo funciona una lengua y cómo cambia en diferentes situaciones. En relación a un estudiante bilingüe, la conciencia metalingüística se refiere a la comprensión de las similitudes y diferencias entre los dos idiomas.

D

dictado (*dictation*) Estrategia de enseñanza en la que el maestro dicta palabras u oraciones relacionadas con los textos o destrezas que los estudiantes están aprendiendo; a lo largo de varios días, los estudiantes abordan el mismo dictado mediante distintas modalidades que refuerzan y amplían todas las competencias lingüísticas (comprensión auditiva, expresión oral, lectura y escritura). El dictado puede usarse como herramienta de apoyo para el desarrollo del lenguaje y de destrezas específicas. En un programa de biliteracidad, también puede usarse para hacer conexiones interlingüísticas.

E

efectividad (*efficacy*) Eficacia; facultad de alcanzar un objetivo; término que describe el hecho de que se obtienen mejores resultados mediante programas de lenguaje dual y de biliteracidad en comparación con una enseñanza exclusivamente en inglés.

equidad (*equity*) Igualdad y justicia; en educación, se refiere al acceso equitativo de todos los estudiantes a una enseñanza eficaz centrada en el estudiante y a materiales adecuados de alta calidad, independientemente del idioma de enseñanza.

evidencia (*evidence*) Información confiable basada en la investigación científica que se incorpora a las decisiones relacionadas con la enseñanza.

F

falsos cognados (*false cognates*) Pares de palabras que suenan y/o se escriben de forma similar en dos idiomas, por lo que se perciben como similares. En cambio, tienen significados diferentes, lo que puede dar lugar a confusiones; también conocidos como *falsos amigos*.

H

hablante de herencia (*heritage speaker*) Estudiante cuya primera lengua es la lengua mayoritaria, pero que ha crecido en un hogar o entorno en el que se habla la lengua asociada. En general, los hablantes de herencia tienen algunas destrezas lingüísticas recesivas y expresivas en la lengua asociada, pero su lengua dominante es la lengua mayoritaria y han recibido su educación formal en ella.

L

lector/escritor emergente (*emergent reader/ writer*) Lector/escritor que se encuentra en la etapa inicial de la adquisición de las destrezas de lectura y escritura.

lengua asociada (*partner language*) Idioma adicional que se enseña en un programa bilingüe; el idioma que no es la lengua mayoritaria.

lengua mayoritaria (*majority language*) Lengua que utiliza la mayor parte de la población de un país determinado.

lengua minoritaria (*minority language*) Lengua que se usa en un país determinado, distinta de la que usa la mayor parte de la población.

M

modelo educativo 50:50 (*50:50 model*) Tipo de programa de lenguaje dual en el que la enseñanza se brinda en la lengua asociada y en la lengua mayoritaria en proporciones iguales en todos los grados.

modelo educativo 90:10 (*90:10 model*) Tipo de programa de lenguaje dual en el que la enseñanza se brinda en la lengua asociada en una proporción del 90 por ciento y, a continuación, en la lengua mayoritaria en una proporción del 10 por ciento durante el primer o los dos primeros años, con un aumento paulatino anual de la cantidad de lengua mayoritaria usada hasta llegar a una proporción del 50:50 entre ambos idiomas, generalmente en el tercer grado.

O

ortografía transparente (*transparent ortography*) Correlación directa entre patrones fonológicos y ortográficos, característica de idiomas como el español, a diferencia de la correspondencia más compleja (u "opaca") entre grafemas y fonemas que poseen otros idiomas, como el inglés.

P

programa bidireccional (*two-way bilingual program*) Programa en el que se enseña tanto en la lengua mayoritaria como en la lengua asociada. Existe una proporción equitativa entre los estudiantes del programa que hablan la lengua asociada y aquellos que hablan la lengua mayoritaria.

programa de biliteracidad secuencial (*sequential biliteracy program*) Programa de inmersión en el que los estudiantes primero reciben la mayor parte de la enseñanza en una lengua y luego adquieren la segunda lengua gradualmente, a medida que avanzan a los grados superiores.

Glosario de términos profesionales *(cont.)*

programa de biliteracidad simultánea *(simultaneous biliteracy program)* Programa de inmersión en el que los estudiantes aprenden en dos idiomas al mismo tiempo desde los primeros grados y a lo largo de toda su educación.

programa de inmersión *(immersion program)* Programa en el que la mayor parte o la totalidad de la enseñanza se realiza en la segunda (o tercera) lengua de los estudiantes. El término *inmersión dual* a veces se usa como sinónimo de *lenguaje dual*.

programa de lenguaje dual *(dual language program)* Programa educativo de largo plazo cuyo objetivo es alcanzar la lectoescritura académica plena en dos idiomas (generalmente la lengua mayoritaria y una lengua asociada). Gran parte de la enseñanza se brinda en ambos idiomas en todas las materias del currículo. Aunque existen muchos modelos de lenguaje dual, todos ellos están diseñados para extenderse por varios años y tienen como objetivo lograr la biliteracidad plena, así como rigurosos logros académicos para todos los estudiantes.

programa de salida *(exit program)* Programa que brinda apoyo en la lengua nativa solo como un paso intermedio para adquirir una segunda lengua; programa que no tiene como objetivo la lectoescritura plena en la lengua nativa, sino que se usa como salida de la lengua nativa para enfocarse en la segunda lengua. En Estados Unidos, los programas bilingües de "salida temprana" se diseñan de forma que los estudiantes tengan una transición de la lengua nativa hacia la lengua mayoritaria lo más rápido posible; los programas de "salida tardía" suelen brindar varios años de apoyo bilingüe. Los programas de lenguaje dual pueden considerarse como programas bilingües "de no salida" (que, idealmente, duran hasta el duodécimo grado o una instancia educativa superior), cuyo objetivo es la biliteracidad plena. Los programas de salida también se denominan *programas de transición*.

programa unidireccional *(one-way bilingual program)* Programa en el que todos los estudiantes son hablantes de una segunda lengua, a diferencia del modelo bidireccional, en el que aproximadamente la mitad de los estudiantes son hablantes de la lengua mayoritaria y la otra mitad son hablantes de la lengua asociada; también se denomina *programa de inmersión en idioma extranjero*.

puente interlingüístico *(cross-linguistic bridging)* Estrategia usada en las clases de enseñanza bilingüe, lenguaje dual y biliteracidad en la que el maestro involucra a los estudiantes en la práctica del análisis lingüístico contrastivo, gracias al cual desarrollan una conciencia metalingüística, a la vez que los anima a transferir contenidos aprendidos en un idioma al otro.

T

transferencia *(transfer)* Capacidad de un hablante de aplicar sus conocimientos sobre los sonidos y la sintaxis de un idioma para leer, escribir y hablar en otro idioma; la transferencia puede ser positiva o negativa; la transferencia negativa puede interferir en la adquisición de la segunda lengua.

translenguaje *(translanguaging)* Prácticas discursivas de individuos bilingües o multilingües que aprovechan todo su repertorio lingüístico. El translenguaje se caracteriza por la integración de varios idiomas en el mismo contexto lingüístico, de un modo que generalmente demuestra la existencia de conciencia metalingüística. Se considera que el translenguaje empodera a los estudiantes y los anima a adueñarse de sus herramientas lingüísticas.

V

variantes léxicas *(lexical variations)* Diferentes palabras que expresan el mismo significado y que son usadas por los hablantes de un mismo idioma provenientes de distintas regiones o entornos.

Análisis lingüístico contrastivo

A los maestros les resultará útil aprender aquellas características específicas de cada idioma que suelen causar dificultades a los estudiantes con otra lengua materna, de modo que puedan brindarles práctica adicional según sea necesario. Los puentes interlingüísticos que se trabajan semanalmente en *¡Arriba la Lectura!* constituyen un buen ejemplo de cómo abordar el análisis lingüístico contrastivo.

El **análisis lingüístico contrastivo** se refiere a la práctica de estudiar de manera conjunta las características lingüísticas de dos idiomas. El análisis lingüístico contrastivo se enfoca sobre todo en cuatro campos lingüísticos: la fonología, la morfología, la sintaxis (gramática) y la pragmática. A fin de que los maestros enseñen con eficacia las similitudes y las diferencias entre los idiomas, es conveniente que hagan **puentes interlingüísticos** en los que enseñen de forma explícita las características de ambos idiomas.

A medida que los estudiantes bilingües van desarrollando sus destrezas lingüísticas, comienzan a integrar estructuras de ambos idiomas en su repertorio lingüístico. Esta integración se denomina translenguaje. El **translenguaje** se caracteriza por el uso de varios idiomas en la misma oración, frase o contexto lingüístico. Es una decisión espontánea que toman los hablantes bilingües en cada momento al usar todos sus recursos lingüísticos para comunicarse con eficacia. Puede ocurrir en la expresión oral, la lectura o la escritura.

Algunas estrategias para promover el translenguaje son ofrecer textos y recursos en ambos idiomas, formar grupos de hablantes heterogéneos, brindar una enseñanza basada en proyectos y clarificar lo enseñado en ambos idiomas.

El propósito del puente interlingüístico es mostrar a los estudiantes las conexiones entre el español y el inglés mediante el análisis lingüístico contrastivo.

Español	Inglés
Tengo hambre.	I am hungry.

En un entorno bilingüe, los estudiantes necesitan un espacio para poner en práctica todo su repertorio lingüístico.

¡Viva el español!

Análisis lingüístico contrastivo (cont.)

Conexiones lingüísticas

Entre idiomas diferentes, pueden existir **similitudes lingüísticas** en distintas áreas, como la fonología, la morfología y la sintaxis. Las similitudes lingüísticas permiten poner en funcionamiento los conocimientos del idioma propio en beneficio del aprendizaje de otra lengua. Por ello, es probable que faciliten la adquisición de la lectura y la escritura en una segunda lengua.

Algunos elementos comunes del español y el inglés a tener en cuenta son los conceptos de lo impreso (la direccionalidad, las palabras, las oraciones y los propósitos de la escritura) y la escritura alfabética. Además, las destrezas de razonamiento y la comprensión del registro lingüístico (lenguaje formal e informal) son destrezas que se transfieren entre el español y el inglés.

En el momento de planificar las lecciones de los puentes interlingüísticos que se enfoquen en las similitudes lingüísticas, es importante considerar en qué se parecen las estructuras lingüísticas de ambos idiomas.

En cambio, las **diferencias lingüísticas** entre los idiomas pueden crear dificultades para la adquisición de la segunda lengua. Por ejemplo, los estudiantes de un segundo idioma a menudo pronuncian las palabras de la nueva lengua según las reglas fonológicas de su idioma primario.

A la hora de enseñar las lecciones de los puentes interlingüísticos entre español e inglés, es fundamental tener en cuenta aspectos tales como las reglas gramaticales, las estructuras de las oraciones, los fonemas y la pragmática, que son diferentes en ambos idiomas, y abordarlos de forma explícita.

Las similitudes y las diferencias lingüísticas entre los idiomas son igualmente importantes en la enseñanza a estudiantes bilingües.

Algunos aspectos para comparar y contrastar

A continuación, se muestra un esquema de las principales similitudes y diferencias entre las lenguas española e inglesa:

Español

- 22 a 24 fonemas/29 letras
- *ñ, h* muda
- La enseñanza de la lectura comienza con las vocales.
- Correspondencia uno a uno entre los fonemas y los grafemas de las vocales
- La división en sílabas es fundamental para aprender a leer.
- Predominan los patrones ortográficos regulares y predecibles.
- Acento ortográfico (tilde)

Ambos

- Conceptos de lo impreso
- Escritura alfabética
- Destrezas de razonamiento
- Registro lingüístico

Inglés

- 44 fonemas/26 letras
- La enseñanza de la lectura comienza con las consonantes.
- La división en sílabas se enseña en las lecciones de conciencia fonológica.
- Los patrones ortográficos irregulares son muy comunes.
- Se enseñan palabras de uso frecuente como apoyo para la fluidez.

La conciencia metalingüística

Ayudar a los estudiantes a entender las similitudes y las diferencias lingüísticas entre dos idiomas facilita la adquisición de ambas lenguas. Además, permite desarrollar la **conciencia metalingüística,** es decir, la comprensión sobre el lenguaje en sí mismo. Esto predispone a los estudiantes a seguir explorando el lenguaje durante toda la vida.

Las tablas de análisis lingüístico contrastivo que aparecen en las siguientes páginas resumen algunos de los principales conceptos de cada campo lingüístico.

¡VIVA EL ESPAÑOL!

Desarrollo del lenguaje en español

Apoyo para los estudiantes que aprenden español como segunda lengua

Estructuras gramaticales La siguiente tabla detalla algunos de los retos más comunes para los estudiantes angloparlantes a la hora de aprender español. Se trata de estructuras y usos que no se transfieren del inglés, por lo que pueden provocar interferencias al aprender español.

Todos estos temas se tratan en las lecciones y en las secciones de "Puente interlingüístico" de este programa, pero las sugerencias servirán para reforzar los temas a lo largo de todo el año con elementos de ayuda visual y actividades que el maestro puede llevar a cabo en cualquier momento.

RETO	SUGERENCIAS PARA LA ENSEÑANZA
Me gusta	Es común que los angloparlantes digan por error: *Yo me gusta* o *Yo gusta*. Haga juegos orales con la **estructura me gusta**. Pida a los estudiantes que formen un círculo y completen la oración *A mí me gusta _____*. Pídales que repitan la oración de todos los compañeros con un turno anterior en el círculo. Repita estas actividades cuando surja el tema en clase.
Paso del tiempo	**En español se utilizan los verbos *hacer* y *llevar* para indicar el paso del tiempo,** por ejemplo: *Hace un año que vine aquí. Llevamos un año aquí.* Estas estructuras no existen en inglés y pueden constituir un reto para los estudiantes. Practique estas estructuras con los estudiantes siempre que surja en clase la oportunidad de hablar del paso del tiempo. Para ello, use estas oraciones incompletas: *Hace _____ que _____. Llevo _____.*
Género de los sustantivos	**En inglés, los sustantivos no tienen género, pero en español, sí.** Para ayudar a los estudiantes a recordar el género de los sustantivos, identifique todos los objetos del salón de clases con etiquetas que incluyan el artículo y el sustantivo, por ejemplo: *la mesa, la silla, el pizarrón, el libro*. Siempre que presente en clase sustantivos nuevos en español, use el artículo delante para reforzar el género del sustantivo. Explique a los estudiantes que, en general, las palabras que llevan *el* delante son masculinas y las que llevan *la* delante son femeninas. Diga que, normalmente, la mayor parte de los nombres de cosas que terminan en *-o* u *-or* son masculinas, mientras que las que terminan en *-a*, *-dad*, *-ción* o *-sión* son femeninas, aunque hay excepciones. Comente que, con algunos sustantivos que hacen referencia a personas, la misma palabra se usa para el masculino o femenino y solo cambia *el* y *la*, por ejemplo: *el estudiante, la estudiante*. Coloque en el salón un cartel con dos columnas: *Femenino* y *Masculino*. Vayan escribiendo bajo el encabezado correspondiente las palabras que los estudiantes vayan aprendiendo.

RETO	SUGERENCIAS PARA LA ENSEÑANZA
Mayúsculas	Explique a los estudiantes que muchas mayúsculas se usan de la misma manera en inglés y en español, pero que en algunos casos no se usan igual. Por ejemplo, **en español, los meses del año y los días de la semana se escriben con minúscula**, a menos que vayan al principio de una oración o sean un encabezado: *lunes, domingo, febrero, septiembre.* **Los idiomas también se escriben con minúscula:** *español, inglés, chino.* Coloque en el salón un cartel con los días de la semana y los meses del año en español e inglés, con las mayúsculas y minúsculas subrayadas. Recuerde a los estudiantes que consulten el cartel cuando vayan a escribir estas palabras. Asegúrese de escribir *español* e *inglés* con minúscula siempre que pueda para repasar estas normas.
Posesión	**En español, se indica posesión con la siguiente estructura:** *la casa de Pablo, el libro de María.* Practique esta estructura con los estudiantes si observa que tienen dificultades para indicar posesión.
Pronombres posesivos	**En español, se tiende a utilizar los pronombres posesivos menos que en inglés en lo que se refiere a las partes del cuerpo y las prendas de ropa.** Si los estudiantes usan oraciones como *Ella levanta su mano*, responda diciéndoles: *Ella levanta la mano.* Asegúrese de utilizar la misma estructura cuando dé instrucciones a los estudiantes: *Levanten la mano. Pónganse la chaqueta.*
Comparaciones	**Para las comparaciones en español**, en lugar de cambiar la terminación del adjetivo como ocurre en inglés, **se utiliza la siguiente estructura: *El perro es más grande que el ratón. El elefante es el más grande de todos.*** Pida a los estudiantes que comparen objetos del salón de clases usando oraciones para completar como: *El lápiz es _____ el libro. El pizarrón es _____ que el cuaderno.*
Conjugaciones verbales	**En español, hay muchas más conjugaciones verbales** que en inglés, por lo que los estudiantes angloparlantes necesitarán práctica para aprender a conjugar los verbos. Coloque en el salón un cartel con los verbos regulares *hablar, comer* y *escribir.* Escriba las terminaciones *-ar, -er, -ir* de otro color. Debajo de cada verbo, escriba las personas y las conjugaciones correctas en el presente, separando la raíz y la terminación del verbo. Los estudiantes pueden usar las terminaciones para conjugar otros verbos terminados en *-ar, -er, -ir.* A medida que los estudiantes vayan progresando en el aprendizaje del español, añada listas de las terminaciones correspondientes a otros tiempos verbales para que los estudiantes las puedan consultar.

Desarrollo del lenguaje en español (cont.)

RETO	SUGERENCIAS PARA LA ENSEÑANZA
Concordancia en género y número de los adjetivos y sustantivos; posición de los adjetivos	En inglés, no existe la **concordancia en género y número de los sustantivos y adjetivos.** Por lo tanto, los estudiantes angloparlantes necesitan practicar este tema. Cree tarjetas de palabras con sustantivos variados y con adjetivos en su forma masculina singular. Luego, pida a los estudiantes que elijan un sustantivo y un adjetivo y que digan una oración con ambas palabras. Deben modificar el adjetivo en forma masculina y singular según haga falta. Escriba los pares de sustantivos y adjetivos correctos en el pizarrón y señale la terminación que indica género y número. Pregunte a los estudiantes dónde va el adjetivo. *(después del sustantivo)*
Sujeto tácito	**En español, muchas veces se omite el sujeto** porque queda implícito en la conjugación del verbo, por ejemplo: *Como una manzana.* Pregunte a los estudiantes: *¿Quién come la manzana?* Si tienen dificultades para decir que es el propio hablante *(yo)*, explique que se deben fijar en la terminación del verbo *(-o)*. Diga que la terminación les servirá para saber quién es el sujeto de la oración, o quién está llevando a cabo la acción de la oración. Aclare que algunas terminaciones corresponden a varios sujetos, como en *(ellos, ustedes) hablan*. Proporcione a los estudiantes distintas oraciones, como: *Corremos en el parque. Caminaste a casa. Hablan con el maestro. Comemos una naranja.* Pídales que indiquen quién está llevando a cabo la acción en cada caso: *yo, tú, él o ella, nosotros, ustedes o ellos o ellas.* Dígales que consulten las terminaciones verbales en los carteles si es necesario. A medida que los estudiantes vayan progresando en el aprendizaje del español, añada otras oraciones con otros tiempos verbales.
Sustantivos generales o abstractos	Diga a los estudiantes que, **en español, se utilizan las palabras *el* o *la, los* o *las* en muchas ocasiones** en que en inglés no se usan. Por ejemplo, escriba en el pizarrón: *Las manzanas son deliciosas.* Señale que, cuando se está hablando de un objeto en general, en este caso todas las manzanas, en español se utilizan los artículos *el* o *la, los* o *las* delante.

Retos fonológicos

En la siguiente tabla, se ofrecen sugerencias para que los estudiantes angloparlantes practiquen la pronunciación de los sonidos nuevos o desconocidos que existen en el idioma español. Estos aspectos de la pronunciación también se tratan en el transcurso de las lecciones y en las secciones de "Puente interlingüístico" de este programa, pero conviene reforzar estos temas durante todo el año.

Tenga siempre en cuenta la importancia de no centrar sus esfuerzos en corregir la pronunciación; si usted focaliza la atención en el significado, los estudiantes generalmente irán adaptando su pronunciación para lograr que los demás los entiendan.

SONIDO	EJEMPLOS	SUGERENCIAS PARA LA ENSEÑANZA
/a/ /e/ /i/ /o/ /u/	abeja, elefante, iguana, oso, uñas	Aunque **las vocales en español no suponen mayores dificultades**, es importante que los estudiantes las practiquen para que se limiten a pronunciar los **cinco sonidos** de forma uniforme, excluyendo otros sonidos de vocales del inglés. Enseñe y cante con los estudiantes versos de canciones populares, como "La pájara pinta". Una vez que sepan la canción, deben cantarla cambiando todas las vocales a una sola, por ejemplo: *Estaba la pájara pinta* *a la sombra de un verde limón,* *con las alas cortaba las hojas,* *con el pico cortaba la flor.* Con la *a*: *Astaba la pájara panta* *a la sambra da an varda lamán,* *can las alas cartaba las hajas,* *can al paca cartaba la flar.* Con la *e*: *Estebe le péjere pente...* Preste especial atención a la letra *e*, ya que muchos estudiantes angloparlantes pueden confundirla con la letra *e* en inglés, que se pronuncia como la *i* en español. Asegúrese de que los estudiantes identifiquen la letra *e* con su sonido correcto.
/ñ/	niño, pequeño, ñame	**El sonido que representa la letra ñ no existe en inglés.** Practique el siguiente trabalenguas con los estudiantes: *Niña ñoña añoñada, añoñado niño ñoño.*
/rr/	perro, carro, rápido	Los estudiantes pueden tener dificultades para pronunciar **el sonido /rr/, que no existe en inglés**. Practique los siguientes trabalenguas con los estudiantes: *Erre con erre cigarra,* *erre con erre barril,* *rápido corren los carros por los rieles del ferrocarril.* *El perro de Roque no tiene rabo* *porque Ramón Ramírez se lo ha robado.* *Y al perro de Ramón Ramírez, ¿quién el rabo le ha robado?*
/r/	claro, coro, caro	**El sonido que representa la r cuando está en el medio o al final de una palabra** puede presentar dificultades para los estudiantes. Muéstreles la posición de la lengua. Pídales que practiquen los sonidos /r/ y /rr/ comparando pares de palabras como *cero, cerro; caro, carro; pero, perro; para, parra.*

Desarrollo del lenguaje en español (cont.)

SONIDO	EJEMPLOS	SUGERENCIAS PARA LA ENSEÑANZA
/j/	**júbilo, gente, girasol, jota**	Los estudiantes pueden tener dificultades para recordar que **el sonido de la _j_ y de la _g_ antes de _e_ o _i_ es igual para las dos letras** y, además, es distinto a los sonidos de esas letras en inglés. Practique los siguientes trabalenguas con los estudiantes. Antes de empezar, siempre muestre o escriba la letra _j_ y enfatice su sonido: _En un juncal de Junqueira,_ _juncos juntaba Julián._ _Juntóse Juan a juntarlos y juntos juncos juntaron._ Antes de empezar, siempre muestre o escriba la letra _g_ y enfatice su sonido: _¡Qué ingenuo es Eugenio! ¡Y qué genio tiene el ingenuo Eugenio!_
combinaciones consonánticas	**grito, trabajo, prado, creo**	Practique estos trabalenguas con los estudiantes: _Tres tristes tigres tragan trigo en un trigal._ _Me trajo Tajo tres trajes, tres trajes me trajo Tajo._ _Contigo entró un tren con trigo, un tren con trigo contigo entró._

Guía rápida para la pronunciación de las vocales en español

Practique las vocales en español con los estudiantes siempre que pueda. Use rimas y canciones con las letras a, _e, i, o, u_ para reforzar la pronunciación de estos cinco sonidos. Pídales que se fijen en la posición de la boca y de los labios mientras pronuncia las letras.

VOCAL	PRONUNCIACIÓN EN ESPAÑOL
a	_a_ as in _father_
e	_e_ as in _elephant_
i (y)	_i_ as in _kid_
o	_o_ as in _October_
u	_u_ as in _flute_

English Language Development

Support for Students Learning English as a Second Language

Teacher Note

This section provides teaching suggestions for teachers of students who are learning English.

Grammar and Sentence Structures The chart below lists some common challenges for Spanish-speaking students learning English as a second language. There are structures in English that do not transfer from Spanish, and they can interfere with the acquisition of English. These topics are addressed in the main lessons and Cross-Linguistic Bridges of this program, but the tips will be helpful in reinforcing these topics throughout the whole year, with visual aids and activities that can be conducted at any time.

CHALLENGE	TEACHING TIPS
Contractions	**There are no contractions for verbs in Spanish,** so students may fail to recognize them in oral conversation in English. Place an anchor chart in the classroom listing the most common contractions and their extended forms (*I'm, we're, you're, he's, she's, can't, don't, won't, isn't, wasn't, didn't*). When a contraction is said in the classroom or read out aloud in a book, point to its spelling on the chart and ask a volunteer for the meaning of the contraction.
Comparative Adjectives	**Students may not be familiar with comparative adjectives,** as comparisons in Spanish are expressed in a different way. Write three columns on the board with the words *warm, warmer, warmest* and underline the ending of each one. Have students brainstorm places that are warm and decide which one is *warm, warmer,* and *warmest*. Repeat with animals and size, and with other items and qualities.
Possessive Pronouns	**In Spanish, the possessive pronoun *su* does not vary according to the gender of the owner,** so students may have more difficulty saying the pronouns *his* and *her* with the correct agreement. They may tend to have the pronoun agree with the object instead of the owner of the object. Distribute cards with the words *his* and *her* on them. Use these sentence frames for practice: *This is Amy. This is _____ book. This is Ryan. This is _____ bag.* Ask students to use the correct card to complete each sentence frame and to tell why they chose it.
Subject Pronouns	**Spanish-speaking students may omit subject pronouns** because they are unnecessary in Spanish. Notice when students omit the pronoun, for example: *Mom is not home. Is at work.* Ask the student: *Who is at work?* When they answer *Mom*, tell them that in English, they must say the subject, or who is performing the action, in every sentence (except in commands such as *Go home*). Otherwise, the sentence is incomplete and we do not know who performed the action. Provide some examples for students to correct in pairs, such as: *I am not hungry. Am thirsty.; They are not here. Are there.*

English Language Development (cont.)

CHALLENGE	TEACHING TIPS
Double Negatives	**Double negatives are correct in Spanish**, so Spanish-speaking students may use them erroneously in English. Write on the board: *I do not need _____.* Ask students to suggest a word to finish the sentence. If they say *nothing*, go back to the sentence and underline the word *not*. Tell them that in English, we do not use two negative words such as *not, no,* or *nothing* in the same sentence. Tell them they can say: *I need nothing* or *I do not need anything.* Explain that *I do not need nothing* is not an option. Keep a visible list of negative words on an anchor chart in the room.
Adjective Placement	**Spanish-speaking students may place the adjective after the noun** because of adjective placement in Spanish. Play a "silly sentences" game to practice using adjectives. Write out a sentence on the board with typical adjectives: *I see green leaves.* Have students find and replace the adjective with a silly one and say or write out the new sentence: *I see blue leaves.*
Pronoun *it*	**Spanish-speaking students are used to referring to objects with masculine or feminine pronouns according to their gender.** Use the following sentence frames for practice. Distribute cards with the words *him, her, it.* Then write or say the following sentence frame pairs: *Give me the pencil. I need _____.; Maria was there. I talked to _____.; My father was home. I said hello to _____.* Ask students: *Him, her, or it?* Have them match up the correct card with each sentence pair. In pairs, have them explain why they picked the pronoun. If necessary, point out that words like *he, she, him,* and *her* are only used to refer to people (and sometimes animals), and that *it* is always used for objects.
Helping Verbs in Questions and Negative Statements	**Spanish-speaking students may be unfamiliar with the use in English of helping verbs in questions and negative statements.** Write some questions and statements on large strips of poster board, for example: *Carl does not eat chocolate. Caiti is not coming to school. Do you want to come?* Then cut up the sentences into words. Have students work in pairs to put the words back together in the correct order. Tell them to use all of the words provided for each sentence.

Phonological Challenges The following chart offers tips for Spanish-speaking students to be able to practice the pronunciation of new or unfamiliar consonant sounds that exist in the English language and do not transfer from Spanish. These aspects of pronunciation are also addressed in the lessons and Cross-Linguistic Bridges in this program. Note that it is important not to overcorrect students' pronunciation; if you keep the emphasis on making meaning, students will generally adjust their pronunciation to be understood.

SOUND	EXAMPLES	TEACHING TIPS
/h/	house, have, hole	**Spanish-speaking students may omit the sound of h in some words,** because the letter h is silent in Spanish. Explain to students that the letter h in English has a sound similar to j in Spanish, in words such as *jinete* and *José*, although it is a softer sound. Use cognates to teach students how to pronounce h in English. For example, write the words *hotel* and *hospital* on the board and read them. Then, ask students to repeat after you.
/dz/	January, jet, just	**Spanish-speaking students may confuse the /dz/ sound** as in *jacket* with the /j/ as in *yacht*, or with the sound that the letter j stands for in Spanish. Have students practice the following rhyme at any time: *Jack be nimble, Jack be quick, Jack jump over the candle-stick.* Make sure to associate the letter j with the initial sound in *Jack* and *jump* by writing it on the board or showing a letter card before starting the rhyme.
/r/	rabbit, right, rose	Have students practice the following song to reinforce **the sound /r/**, which does not transfer from Spanish. Make sure to associate the letter r with the initial sound in *row* by writing it on the board or showing a letter card before starting the rhyme: *Row, row, row your boat* *Gently down the stream,* *Merrily, merrily, merrily, merrily,* *Life is but a dream.*
/v/	victory, voice, have	**Spanish speakers may have trouble differentiating the /v/ from the /b/ sound,** because there is no distinction between those sounds in Spanish. Say pairs of words with b and v, such as *ban/van, bet/vet, lob/love,* emphasizing the /b/ and /v/ sounds. Ask students to focus on the difference in your lips when you say each of the pairs. Have students say and repeat the sound. Then, distribute letter cards for b and v. Say the words in random order and have students hold up the card for the correct letter.
/z/	dozen, zoo	**The sound /z/ does not exist in Spanish,** so students may need extra practice to hear it and reproduce it. Use sound and spelling cards with images to practice pronouncing words with the /z/ sound. Have students repeat the words at first. When they are ready for more practice, have students use them in conversation.

¡Viva el español!

English Language Development *(cont.)*

Sounds Represented by Blends and Digraphs

SOUND	EXAMPLES	TEACHING TIPS
/ŋ/ /nk/ /rk/ /rm/	something, bank, park, norm	**Spanish-speaking students may tend to leave off consonant blends at the end of words,** which do not exist in Spanish. Make sure to pronounce the end sounds of words clearly and in an exaggerated way to promote students' understanding of the sounds. Encourage students to "keep going" and prolong the end sounds of words they are having difficulty with.
/ʃ/	should, show, rush	**Many Spanish-speaking students are not familiar with the ʃ sound** and may confuse it with the closest sound they know in Spanish, which is /tʃ/ as in *chair*. Constantly emphasize the difference in pronunciation between /ʃ/ and /tʃ/. In pairs, have students practice reading to each other pairs of words such as *sheep, cheap; shoes, choose.* Model the sound first and emphasize the difference in the two sounds. Encourage students to pronounce each word slowly.
/ø/	think, thread, ethical	Have students practice the following jingle to reinforce the **sound /ø/** as in *think*, which does not transfer from Spanish:* *Three blind mice. Three blind mice.* *See how they run. See how they run.*
/ð/	them, those, although	Have students practice the following rhyme to reinforce the **sound /ð/** as in *that*, which does not transfer from Spanish: *This little piggy went to market,* *this little piggy stayed at home,* *this little piggy had popcorn,* *this little piggy had none.* *And this little piggy went...* *Wee wee wee all the way home.*
/w/	white, where, who	Have students practice the following tongue-twister to reinforce the **sound /w/** as in *when*, which does not transfer from Spanish: *Whether the weather be fine,* *Or whether the weather be not,* *Whether the weather be cold,* *Or whether the weather be hot,* *We'll weather the weather* *Whatever the weather,* *Whether we like it or not!*

* *Except for the variant spoken in most of Spain, where the letters* **c** *(with* **e** *and* **i***) and* **z** *stand for a sound similar to /th/ in the word* **think.**

Fundamentos teóricos

Introducción

En el ciclo 2014–2015, se estimaba que unos 4.6 millones de escolares en Estados Unidos eran aprendices del idioma inglés (ELL, por sus siglas en inglés). La mayoría de ellos (77.1%), provenían de hogares de habla hispana. Según las investigaciones, solo el 63% de estos se gradúan de la escuela secundaria y la mayoría asiste a escuelas de bajo rendimiento[1].

Existen cuatro tipos de programas para estudiantes ELL:

- **SEI** (*Sheltered English Inmersion*) Clases que brindan contenido específico para ELL en inglés, antes de la transición a la enseñanza tradicional, que también es solo en inglés.

- **ESL** (*English as a Second Language*) Clases especializadas impartidas por un maestro capacitado en la enseñanza del inglés como segunda lengua, para promover las destrezas de adquisición del idioma. Pueden dictarse a todo el grupo o a una selección de estudiantes.

- **TBE** (*Transitional Bilingual Education*) Programas de transición bilingües que ofrecen de dos a tres años de enseñanza en el idioma nativo antes de hacer la transición a las clases tradicionales en inglés.

- **DLI** (*Dual Language Inmersion*) Programas de inmersión en los dos idiomas que brindan enseñanza en el idioma nativo y en el segundo idioma en paralelo. La frecuencia puede ser diaria, semanal o quincenal, según el programa.

Se espera que los participantes de los programas TBE y DLI desarrollen gradualmente las destrezas en su lengua nativa y apliquen esos conceptos a la segunda lengua (o lengua asociada) que están aprendiendo[2]. Thomas y Collier (2017) informan de que, luego de cursar en programas de escolarización bilingües durante siete años, los aprendices de inglés latinos progresan más en inglés cada año que los estudiantes que hablan inglés como única lengua y asisten a programas tradicionales. Y es por eso que, para el séptimo grado, los latinos y los aprendices de inglés logran cerrar la brecha y alcanzar el mismo nivel que quienes estudian solo en inglés[3].

Hoy hay más estudiantes inscritos en programas bilingües (TBE y DLI) que nunca. A medida que más investigaciones demuestren los beneficios de aprender otro idioma, estos programas continuarán desarrollándose y multiplicándose. Los programas bilingües en Estados Unidos están dirigidos a estudiantes de inglés como segundo idioma y a estudiantes angloparlantes. Están diseñados para desarrollar el bilingüismo y la biliteracidad en todos los estudiantes, sin importar su trasfondo lingüístico. Todos los programas bilingües requieren textos escritos por autores nativos, materiales didácticos multiculturales relevantes y destrezas fundamentales para el aprendizaje del español. *¡Arriba la Lectura!* no solo cumple este cometido, sino que nuestros autores han diseñado un plan de estudios de alfabetización holístico y alineado con los estándares de enseñanza.

Por más de 180 años, Houghton Mifflin Harcourt ha estado profundamente comprometido con la literatura y la alfabetización como método para mejorar la vida de las personas. *¡Arriba la Lectura!* continúa esa tradición. Este artículo de investigación explica cómo *¡Arriba la Lectura!* basa su desarrollo en las mejores investigaciones

---

[1] https://nces.ed.gov/fastfacts/display.asp?id=96

[2] https://www.npr.org/sections/ed/2017/02/23/512451228/5-million-english-language-learners-a-vast-pool-of-talent-at-risk

[3] Thomas, W. P. & Collier, V. P. (2017). *Why Dual Language Schooling.* Albuquerque, NM: Dual Language Education of New Mexico – Fuente Press.

Fundamentos teóricos (cont.)

sobre la enseñanza y el aprendizaje del español y la educación bilingüe. En esta sección, se presentan investigaciones relacionadas con el español y el bilingüismo y cómo *¡Arriba la Lectura!* las incorpora.

Panorama general del programa

¡Arriba la Lectura! es un plan de estudios de alfabetización integral que prepara a todos los estudiantes para ser lectores y escritores exitosos. Con un enfoque auténtico para la alfabetización en español, expone a los estudiantes a una variedad de textos escritos por autores nativos de habla hispana, mientras aprenden las destrezas fundamentales de la lengua española. Este programa se puede utilizar en cualquier modelo de enseñanza bilingüe.

La enseñanza básica

La enseñanza básica se basa en un modelo de taller de lectura que incluye textos valiosos presentados en mini lecciones de lectura atenta, con apoyo para los estudiantes en todos los niveles de lectura. Muchos de los textos en español fueron escritos por autores de habla hispana reconocidos en todo el mundo. Se seleccionaron minuciosamente y abarcan una variedad de géneros que incluyen ficción, no ficción, poesía, teatro y otros medios.

El enfoque en el taller de escritura paso a paso proporciona modelos y enseñanza sobre el proceso y la técnica e integra la gramática española dentro del contexto de la escritura. En los primeros grados, la enseñanza sistemática y explícita de las destrezas fundamentales en español se presenta en un modelo gradual con diferenciación en grupos pequeños.

Ventajas de los programas de lenguaje dual

Ser bilingüe confiere a los estudiantes ventajas cognitivas, culturales y sociales. Muchos estudiantes asisten a programas de lenguaje dual para aprender en su idioma nativo mientras agregan una lengua asociada (a veces llamadas L1 y L2). La expectativa es que los estudiantes en programas de calidad lean,

escriban y hablen a un nivel académico alto en ambos idiomas cuando lleguen al quinto grado.

Ventajas cognitivas

Numerosas investigaciones sobre los efectos del bilingüismo demuestran que los estudiantes que aprenden en dos idiomas desarrollan rigurosas destrezas de razonamiento, aplican la lógica a tareas complejas, tienen una mayor tasa de retención en la memoria y están mejor preparados para aprender más idiomas. Las investigaciones indican que los estudiantes que aprenden en dos idiomas muestran mayor neuroplasticidad, o control sobre los procesos cognitivos. Esto se conoce como "ventaja bilingüe" (Costa, Hernández, Costa-Faidella y Sebastián-Gallés, 2009; Scaltritti, Peressotti y Miozzo, 2015). Los estudiantes aprenden a aplicar las destrezas y los conocimientos de un idioma al otro. Además, los estudios demuestran que los estudiantes bilingües de todas las edades adquieren un funcionamiento ejecutivo superior al de los monolingües de la misma edad y con el mismo contexto.

Ventajas culturales

Los programas de lenguaje dual exponen a los estudiantes a las costumbres y tradiciones del idioma que la escuela enseña. Los textos escritos originalmente en español, las celebraciones culturales y las conexiones sólidas entre la escuela y el hogar son fundamentales para la enseñanza bilingüe. Los estudiantes para quienes el idioma de destino es su idioma nativo pueden mantener la conexión con su herencia, mientras que los estudiantes que aprenden el idioma de destino desarrollan competencias interculturales.

Ventajas sociales

Los estudiantes que aprenden dos o más idiomas desarrollan la capacidad de comunicarse y de formar relaciones significativas con personas que provienen de diversas culturas. En los programas de lenguaje dual en los que los estudiantes usan los dos idiomas para interactuar, los estudiantes desarrollan una perspectiva social, ya que deben tomar decisiones conscientes sobre el idioma que usarán para dirigirse a las personas (Hsin, 2017).

Ventajas globales

Las investigaciones demuestran que los estudiantes bilingües tienen ventaja sobre los monolingües a la hora de obtener un puesto de trabajo, para comunicarse y para comprender a compañeros con antecedentes distintos y oportunidades económicas diversas [4]. Los programas bilingües ofrecen a sus estudiantes una forma de convertirse en ciudadanos globales cuando aprenden a ver su educación desde una perspectiva cultural y multilingüe [5].

 En ¡Arriba la Lectura!...

La guía **Lenguaje dual: Guía de implementación** fue creada por la Dra. Elena Izquierdo para ayudar a los maestros a diseñar sus propios programas de lenguaje dual en base a los recursos paralelos de *¡Arriba la Lectura!* e *Into Reading*. Esta guía es un recurso de fácil acceso y consulta permanente para los maestros, con un atractivo diseño que facilita la lectura y la navegación. La **Guía del maestro** de *¡Arriba la Lectura!* incluye también recuadros de "Dual Language Settings" y la sección "Puente interlingüístico" como herramientas adicionales para las clases de lenguaje dual.

 **❝** *Los modelos de lenguaje dual enfatizan la alfabetización académica, no solo el bilingüismo* **❞**.

— Dra. Elena Izquierdo

Contexto de enseñanza en español

¡Arriba la Lectura! fue desarrollado con especial atención a los siguientes principios para la calidad de las artes del lenguaje en español y la enseñanza en dos idiomas:

- La enseñanza del español debe dictarse de acuerdo con las características lingüísticas y las estructuras pedagógicas más adecuadas para el aprendizaje del español.

- Los conocimientos previos de los estudiantes sobre el español se honran y se valoran, mientras que la participación en rigurosos programas académicos bilingües y de lenguaje dual elevan sus destrezas y competencias.

- La mejor forma de aprender para los estudiantes en programas bilingües es a través de planes de estudio multiculturales con textos escritos originalmente en español.

- El aprendizaje debe centrarse en los estudiantes para que se desarrollen más allá de sus competencias académicas, incluidos los factores no cognitivos, el aprendizaje socioemocional y la sensibilidad cultural.

- Leer, escribir, escuchar y hablar son dominios de la alfabetización fundamentalmente relacionados y deben enseñarse con un enfoque que los integre.

---

[4] https://www.aft.org/ae/fall2015/goldenberg_wagner

[5] http://blogs.edweek.org/edweek/global_learning/2018/05/seven_essential_components_for_successful_dual_language_programs.html

¡Viva el español!

Fundamentos teóricos (cont.)

- La enseñanza efectiva se basa en datos y la evaluación es uno de sus componentes esenciales. Las evaluaciones para un programa de lenguaje dual toman en cuenta el desarrollo de los estudiantes bilingües emergentes.

- Las competencias de los estudiantes en inglés y en español se valoran al mismo nivel y se aplican a ambos idiomas para ampliar las destrezas.

- A los estudiantes se les debe motivar para que usen su repertorio lingüístico en ambos idiomas plenamente a través del translenguaje.

- El aprendizaje profesional continuo de los docentes es un componente vital de la educación de calidad.

Destrezas fundamentales del español

Según Jill Kerper Mora, existe una progresión recomendada para aprender español. Primero, los estudiantes deben ser expuestos a las destrezas y conceptos previos a la lectura. Esto incluye distinguir letras, palabras, oraciones y la direccionalidad en los textos impresos. Estas destrezas se consideran transferibles y, cuando se aprenden en español, se pueden aplicar inmediatamente al inglés. Luego, los estudiantes se exponen a las vocales del español y a las consonantes transferibles. Esto sienta las bases para la introducción de la conciencia silábica. El español es un lenguaje silábico[6] y, por ende, los principiantes aprenden a leer dividiendo las palabras en sílabas y luego combinándolas para formar palabras. La enseñanza del orden alfabético y los nombres de las letras debe posponerse hasta que los estudiantes dominen la correspondencia entre letras y sonidos (Mora, 2016). Finalmente, se les enseña a progresar de la lectura de sílabas aisladas a la lectura de palabras completas. Las destrezas fundamentales también deben incluir temas de gramática, como conjugación de verbos, sujetos tácitos y lecciones de ortografía, así como los usos culturales del español.

En ¡Arriba la Lectura!...

A través de la enseñanza explícita y sistemática de sonidos, sílabas y palabras, ¡Arriba la Lectura! desarrolla y refuerza las destrezas básicas de lectura en español. La enseñanza de estrategias de vocabulario y análisis estructural se apoya en la adquisición independiente de palabras por parte de los estudiantes.

El programa aplica la destreza fundamental del día a una selección decodificable a través de las **Lecturas iniciales,** escritas específicamente para la enseñanza del español. Mediante las **Tarjetas de enseñanza,** los **Alfamigos,** las hojas proyectables de **Mostrar y motivar** (con canciones, rimas y poemas escritos originalmente en español) y las **Minilecciones del rotafolio de mesa,** se proporcionan múltiples recursos de enseñanza diseñados para apoyar las destrezas fundamentales en español.

Sistema de sonido del idioma español

El español es un lenguaje muy regular y consistente con una correspondencia individual entre letras y sonidos, lo que crea límites claramente definidos entre sílabas (Beeman y Urow, 2012). La progresión recomendada para enseñar a los estudiantes a leer en español es comenzar con vocales y consonantes transferibles y luego presentarles gradualmente las sílabas. Según la Dra. Elena Izquierdo, "en español la sílaba es fundamental" (2018). Una vez que los estudiantes han demostrado dominio de la combinación de sonidos en sílabas, están listos para progresar a patrones más complejos e intransferibles.

En ¡Arriba la Lectura!...

Las tres primeras semanas de enseñanza fonética en el kínder en ¡Arriba la Lectura! están dedicadas a las vocales, para sentar las bases para la introducción de las sílabas. A partir de la cuarta semana, se presenta a los estudiantes el sonido de una consonante por semana (ocasionalmente dos sonidos) en

[6] Amador-Hernández, M. (1986). Spanish as a "syllable-timed" language. *The Journal of the Acoustical Society of America 80,* S96.

combinación con las cinco vocales. Los sonidos de las letras se presentan progresivamente según la frecuencia de las consonantes para potenciar al máximo las destrezas de decodificación. Los repasos semanales refuerzan los sonidos de las letras aprendidas y el principio alfabético.

Para la semana 30, todos los sonidos han sido ya presentados y se habla del alfabeto explícitamente a través de canciones y actividades. Cada semana, la enseñanza de fonética de 5 días consiste en lo siguiente:

- Los sonidos de las consonantes se enseñan en combinación con las vocales mediante el uso de los personajes de **Alfamigos,** creados específicamente para el español y presentados a través de coloridas tarjetas y videos.

- Se guía a los estudiantes para que busquen palabras en las oraciones usando claves del contexto.

- Las guías de pronunciación facilitan la producción oral en español.

- Se practica la escritura a mano con movimientos cenestésicos y hojas de escritura.

- Se hacen demostraciones y se ofrece práctica individual mediante la formación de palabras con tarjetas de letras y sílabas.

- Se expone a los estudiantes a sonidos, letras y sílabas a través de poemas, rimas y canciones escritas por las autoras F. Isabel Campoy y Alma Flor Ada, así como a canciones populares tradicionales de los países de habla hispana.

- Se practica la lectura coral (palabras y oraciones) con materiales proyectables.

- Se estimula la formación de nuevas palabras utilizando tarjetas de sílabas diseñadas específicamente para el programa en español.

- A partir del final del kínder, se comienzan a escribir palabras u oraciones dictadas.

- Se clasifican palabras e imágenes.

- Se leen y analizan dos cuentos decodificables en español por semana, centrados en las destrezas de fonética y las palabras de uso frecuente de esa semana.

Literatura escrita en español

Los programas bilingües deben proporcionar materiales de enseñanza escritos en su idioma original. La Dra. Elena Izquierdo afirma: "¡La importancia de la alfabetización académica tanto en español como en inglés no se puede enfatizar lo suficiente!" (2018). Los materiales académicos escritos en su idioma original son la base con la que todos los estudiantes se encontrarán y con la que interactuarán durante su día escolar.

Los materiales originales en español abordan las normas y valores culturales del idioma de destino. Esto aporta muchas ventajas a los estudiantes que interactúan con ellos: les brinda una pantalla donde visualizar los valores culturales, el lenguaje social y las personas de las comunidades sobre las que leen. Por ejemplo, la vida en México se vuelve tangible cuando los estudiantes leen sobre dos primos, uno en Estados Unidos y otro en México, y sobre las diferencias y similitudes entre sus vidas. Estos tipos de textos sirven como una conexión directa de los estudiantes con la cultura y las personas de los países cuyo idioma están aprendiendo. Para algunos, esta será la única oportunidad que tengan de "visitar" estos países.

El Consejo Estadounidense para la Enseñanza de Lenguas Extranjeras (ACTFL) afirma que "los materiales originales proporcionan ejemplos de la vida real en los que se utiliza el lenguaje en situaciones cotidianas como una estrategia para captar el interés del estudiante. [...] Los materiales originales pueden proporcionar información sobre la cultura sobre la que se está aprendiendo y proporcionar la perspectiva de

Fundamentos teóricos (cont.)

esa cultura acerca de un tema o evento. La riqueza del lenguaje que se encuentra en los materiales originales proporciona una fuente de lenguaje que los estudiantes de idiomas necesitan para la adquisición"[7]. Además, la lectura de textos escritos por autores nativos de habla hispana brinda acceso y equidad en los recursos y materiales presentados a los estudiantes.

En ¡Arriba la Lectura!...

¡Arriba la Lectura! celebra la riqueza de la literatura hispana. Los textos de autores hispanos representan casi el 60% de los textos de todos los grados e incluyen canciones y cuentos tradicionales, así como textos de autores premiados como Graciela Montes, José Martí, Amado Nervo, Suni Paz, Rubén Darío, Georgina Lázaro, María Elena Walsh y Jorge Urgueta. Los autores de ¡Arriba la Lectura! provienen de una variedad de países de habla hispana, entre ellos México, Puerto Rico, Argentina, España, Cuba, Nicaragua, Chile, Colombia, Ecuador y El Salvador. La **Revista Aventuras** y la sección "Nuestra lengua es arte" cuentan con literatura 100% original que expone a los estudiantes a un vocabulario rico y diverso y a contenidos que representan al mundo de habla hispana.

La **Guía del maestro** de ¡Arriba la Lectura! contiene más obras originales escritas por autores de habla hispana, como los textos decodificables que componen las **Lecturas iniciales;** las hojas proyectables de **Mostrar y motivar,** con canciones, rimas y poemas; y la sección "Extensión lingüística". Creada por la autora del programa y experta en dos idiomas, la Dra. Elena Izquierdo, esta sección se enfoca en la alfabetización académica en español, con actividades de comprensión y vocabulario y oportunidades para conversaciones colaborativas. Además, incluye un "Puente interlingüístico" con sugerencias específicas para conectar el aprendizaje en ambos idiomas dentro de cada módulo.

Asimismo, ¡Arriba la Lectura! ofrece selecciones en los **Libros para la lectura en voz alta,** los **Superlibros** (GK–1) y **miLibro** (G1–6) como conexiones multiculturales auténticas a los países de habla hispana. Las autoras del programa, F. Isabel Campoy y Alma Flor Ada, revisaron minuciosamente todos los poemas, lecturas y selecciones literarias del programa para garantizar que estos textos sean de gran calidad, relevantes culturalmente, con riqueza y naturalidad en el lenguaje y oportunos para los estudiantes bilingües. Supervisaron muy de cerca al talentoso equipo de escritores hispanos de ¡Arriba la Lectura! y contribuyeron con textos literarios a la sección "Extensión lingüística" como oportunidad para promover el aprecio por el idioma, la literatura y la cultura hispana.

Para obtener información más detallada sobre los fundamentos teóricos de ¡Arriba la Lectura!, consulte *Into Reading Research Foundation Paper*.

---

[7] https://www.actfl.org/guiding-principles/use-authentic-texts-language-learning